W9-DGS-357

THE SLUMS

CHALLENGE AND RESPONSE

THE
SLUMS

CHALLENGE
AND
RESPONSE

David R. Hunter

The Free Press

Collier-Macmillan Ltd., London

HV
4045
.H8

Copyright © 1964 by The Free Press of Glencoe

A DIVISION OF THE MACMILLAN COMPANY

Printed in the United States of America

All rights in this book are reserved. No part of this book may be used or reproduced in any manner whatsoever without written permission except in the case of brief quotations embodied in critical articles and reviews.

Second Printing March 1965

For information, address:

The Free Press
A Division of The Macmillan Company
The Crowell-Collier Publishing Company
60 Fifth Avenue, New York, N. Y. 10011

DESIGNED BY FRANK E. COMPARATO

Library of Congress Catalog Card Number: 64-20311

Collier-Macmillan Canada, Ltd., Toronto, Ontario

CONTENTS

Alma College Library
Alma, Michigan

CHAPTER II (*Continued*)

PART TWO

RESPONSE: *What to do About it. Possibilities for Policy and Action*

Prologue

CHAPTER III. *Education*

Chapter III (*Continued*)

Chapter IV. *Economic Self-Sufficiency and Employment*   143

CONTENTS

CHAPTER VII (*Continued*)

INTRODUCTION

This book is about the slum and its people. It attempts to look at them from many perspectives and then to suggest some things that can be done to prevent the continuing formation of slums and to reduce the number existing today.

It very soon becomes clear that one cannot talk about slums without talking about society as a whole. The slum is the result of a variety of forces, events, and deficiencies in our social and economic structure and in our ways of doing things.

Some will say: "The slums have always been with us and always will be. They are part of city life that may be unpleasant but there's not much that can be done about them. They are an inevitable aspect of the urban scene."

No one can *prove* that this is not so, since there is no experience in world history to call up in evidence. Logical analysis, however, does not support the view that slums are "inevitable." That they are extraordinarily difficult to prevent and abolish is all too clear. They represent an extremely complex phenomenon and we simply don't know a precise formula by which they are produced or may be destroyed.

That does not mean we are helpless before the gaze of a

Gorgon, however. We do know some things and have good hunches about others—enough so that a defensible course of action can be plotted. If we fail to plot and follow such a course in the years immediately ahead, we will be in deep trouble.

That is one of the purposes of this book: to amplify and focus the voices that are crying a warning. The slums represent the end product of forces in American society that are divisive and destructive. Even a healthy organism has some such forces at work within it, but when they grow too strong and pervasive the organism sickens. Some of those forces are now growing stronger and will compel a response. Whether the response will be chaotic, uncontrolled, and itself destructive is the question. It need not be.

One thing is sure: Slums will not disappear by themselves. The workings of the "free market" or "natural" evolutionary processes will not eliminate them. It is doubtful that such things exist anyway. Our economic and social lives are now lived out in a skein of rules and regulations and controls and "policies" that very much determine what we may or not do. We may not legally quit school after the fourth grade, for instance. We may not kill ourselves. We may not make noise that disturbs our neighbors. We may not monopolize a market. We must give up part of our income for the general good. The list is long. Yet there is need for some additions to help to establish the conditions and systems which will promote full human development for all people. For at bottom it is incomplete human development that makes slums.

This is not a book for scholars. It is a book for people who have some responsibility or some desire to "do something about it." Hopefully it will be read by political office holders, members of boards of education, members of boards of public and private agencies engaged with one aspect or another of city life, civic leaders, trade union organizers, executive secretaries of chambers of commerce, civil rights leaders, teachers, bureaucrats, social workers, policemen, and housewives.

One month in the slums and I am sad
    So sad
I seem devil possessed
    Or mad

Sweet Heaven sends no miracle to ease
    This hell
The careless earth rings no alarum bell

Is there no way that help can come?

TOYOHIKO KAGAWA
Songs From the Slums

Part **I**

CHALLENGE

*CHARACTERISTICS OF
THE SLUMS AND
WHY THEY ARE
STILL A MAJOR PROBLEM
FOR AMERICA*

CHAPTER I

The Slum
in Perspective

SLUMS ARE ONE of America's major social and economic
problems in the 1960s.

This in spite of the fact that we live in an "affluent society";
in spite of the fact that we have had housing and slum
clearance programs for many years; in spite of the fact that
people have been moving out of the inner city to suburbia.

The slums are still with us and so is poverty. The two
go together, along with assorted other relations, making
for an extremely complicated "multi-problem family" that
threatens the health and viability of the American system. Over
twelve million people live in American urban slums today—
as many as the combined population of Sweden and Denmark.

There are some very potent reasons why national concern with slums has heightened. Slums undermine a democratic system of government. They weaken the international
position of the United States. They starve human talent. They

fail to produce the skilled manpower required to operate an increasingly technical economy. They cost the taxpayers money. They trap people and ensnare them in a way of life that in most cases can hardly be called civilized. They are equivalent to new-world ghettos. They drive vital elements out of the city and exert strong pressures toward deterioration of the city.

Sometimes "image," American's great concern, is regarded as a false value. The complaint is valid when it has to do with an image of high social status derived from the kind of cigarette you smoke or the car you drive. It is not valid when it comes to the image the rest of the world has of a nation.

The image of the United States tolerating or unable to cope with slums is not conducive to the building of full confidence in us by the nations we most wish to influence. This refers particularly to the newer nations whose populations are largely nonwhite. Since the problem of the slums in this country is increasingly compounded by the problem of race, this does not sit well with many of the new nations. They know where Negroes live in America.

To the man on the other side of the table in international councils, our image is tarnished and we are vulnerable because we have yet to deal adequately with slums. His face may be a mask of respect and politeness. But even if his general political orientation disposes him to be a friend there is a doubt in his mind: "These people must either be less clever than they appear, or more cynical. How can we look to them as a model?"

The people of the new nations have two outstanding characteristics: they are poor and they are dark skinned. So, increasingly, are the people of American slums. This cannot but dim the view of us from Africa and Asia.

To see it whole

Most of us know what some aspect of a slum is, but we don't see the total picture. Or if we once did, we may have forgotten it by now. Or we may be busy looking the other way, not wishing to be reminded that the slum is still there and won't go away unless its departure is facilitated.

Apparently this attitude has been around a long time. Eric Partridge notes that the origin of the word slum, although obscure, probably comes from "slumber" since slums were originally "to the majority—unknown, back streets or alleys, wrongly presumed to be sleepy and quiet." [1]

Over the years Webster has softened this view a bit. In 1931 the dictionary said a slum was a foul back street of a city, especially one with a slovenly and often vicious population; a low or squalid neighborhood. In 1953 a more charitable feeling prevailed, and a slum was defined as a thickly populated street or alley marked by squalor or wretched living conditions.

The first part of this book tries to sum up all the things a slum is, so we may better understand the nature of the beast, before moving on to the things that might be done about it. Along with this summary are some opinions about why the facts and the characteristics of the slum still add up to a major, even a critical, problem.

Anybody who tries to sum up all the characteristics of something is bound to get into trouble. Something will be left out. Or something will be put in that somebody else thinks is quite wrong. But one of the declared purposes of this book is to put all these things in, in the belief that they are correct. If they are not, then someone else will be challenged to prove that they are not and, if he succeeds, we will be advanced along the road to improvement.

What to call it

"Slum" is a good, old-fashioned word that carries real meaning. Other terms have been invented to define more precisely different kinds of poor areas, or for euphemistic reasons, or just to get away from tired old words. Some of these are "blighted area," "deteriorated neighborhood," "gray area," "lower class neighborhood," "low income area."

A slum is a cancer in a city. A city that is not making at least partially energetic and effective sorties against its slums is in danger of the slum's metastacizing, and changing the essential character of the city itself.

The cycle

In broad strokes the picture is something like this. Those who can afford it move out of the city proper to the suburbs. Some move back when their children have grown up, but there is not yet a significant mass return, and it is doubtful that there ever will be. Those who move out are those who have better jobs, more money, less skin pigmentation. They pay more taxes and can effectively demand more and better education for their children.

These people are replaced in the city proper by people of lower everything: social status, income, occupational level, education, and future expectations. The replacement is not man for man, since practically all of the large cities lost population from 1950 to 1960. *Metropolitan areas* added population dramatically, but this growth was and is in the peripheral areas—suburbia.

The newcomers move not only to slums but also to "gray areas." A "gray area" is an area in transition, on the way down. It is extensive in many cities. It usually surrounds or is adjacent to the central city and abuts the slum proper. It most likely consists of street after street of closely-packed one- or two-family houses or smaller apartment buildings. In some cases it has larger houses once inhabited by well-to-do people. When an area becomes gray, poorer people move in; often they are members of minority groups, but not always. White migrants to northern cities from the southern Appalachians also make an area gray.

Such an area is recognizable by the fact that it is not very well kept; there are signs in the windows of the houses: "Single Room for Rent"; the larger houses have been taken over by small enterprises such as funeral parlors, beauty shops, and auto parts stores. It has a generally run-down appearance. There are more children in the street, and their skin color is likely to be dark.

In addition to people, much economic activity also moves out of the city, though not all. There are certain kinds of activity, like the garment industry in New York, which, under present methods of doing business, demand a clustering of the elements of the trade. Even in the garment industry, however there is an increasing tendency to dispersal. Financial operations, advertising, and other office-centered enterprise lubricated by frequent face-to-face contact tend to stay in the city. But many large manufacturing and distributing establishments, big taxpayers and employers, are on the way out or have already gone. Whether or not people follow economic activity, or vice versa, is not totally clear. The process probably works both ways.

The city proper begins to have more people with less money, less education, poorer jobs, and more social problems, while the suburbs collect the white, middle class people who are better able to pay for government and public services and who contribute to keeping suburban standards of behavior, education, culture, and physical environment up to par, in accordance with the American dream. Of course, as we know from the myriad books and articles on the ills of suburbia, there are problems at that end of the line as well—but they are not the subject of this book. For our purposes, the suburbs are where most of the people on the way up want to be, and because of this the city proper is drained of resources and talent.

What follows is a downward, self-accelerating spiral for the core of the city, with an increase in blight, crime, dependency, and other familiar problems.

There is a difference between a slum and a gray area, although the line between the two may not always be easily identifiable. A gray area is an area in downward transition. This is where wealthier people used to live. They have now gone to the suburbs, and their houses and apartments are being subdivided to accommodate many more occupants, often people relatively new to the city. It is called "gray" precisely because it's an in-between kind of place, neither a slum nor a high-income, residential zone.

Some people insist on calling a slum a slum in order to avoid the common practice of pretending to solve a problem by changing its name. Dr. James B. Conant is one of these forthright people, who demonstrated this by titling his book,

Slums and Suburbs. He says: "In each one (of the largest American cities) one can find neighborhoods composed of various minority groups. Many of these are areas now designated as "culturally deprived" or "culturally different," but in my youth they would have been more simply designated as "slums." [2]

Through literary eyes

Sometimes a work of literature tells more about what a slum really is than an analytical treatise.

Broadway is one of the longest streets in the world, it's also the ugliest. On a hot humid August morning you see the buildings shimmering. The sky is a steamy gray. The people try to drown themselves with Riker's orange juice. Figueroa lives in the Chester, a building standing next to a Broadway cake shop with cakes in the window that look as though they've been baked in a plastic factory. . . . (The manager of the Chester says) "I wouldn't live in this neighborhood any more if you gave me a penthouse free. This is shot, killed dead. These buildings are rat holes. You need a machine gun in your pocket after six o'clock."

I had grown accustomed to the broken mail boxes where the names piled up like junked cars. The hallways that smelled of urine and pork. But I could never get accustomed to the fat lumbering rats with enlarged stomachs who looked as though they had just swallowed a baby whole.

I knew the building from the face of Mrs. Owens who smoked all brands. She had fifty families in the building. And she carried them like a woman going into her tenth month. The building had been taken over by operators. The great six and eight room apartments were demolished. The kitchens were

turned into community kitchens with a padlock on the refriger-
ator. A coat of green paint buried the old plaster work. The
rooms were filled with families on assistance paying $16 to $25
a week for a room. The view out of the windows was the
Hudson River. But no one ever saw the river. I never heard a
single client mention the river. The Hudson just didn't exist.
The operators of the building were two men who looked as
though they had spent their childhood drowning their playmates. They wrote rent receipts the Supreme Court couldn't
decipher. I'm sure that more care was taken of the garbage
collected in New York than the people in that building. The
building was massive. For me it was always toppling. I could
see it falling into the river. The building had no life, no living
people in it. Not a single person with a plan for tomorrow
morning. And the children in the building raced through the
corridors like wild horses going over a cliff." [3]

Passages like the above give a better "description" of
a slum than many paragraphs of precise and accurate details.
This is because the slum is more than any of its parts, more
than you can see. It is more than the crowded buildings. It is
more than the dirty streets, the lackluster people sitting on
the steps, the shrieking children running up and down, the
sullen boys hanging on the corner, the stupefied addicts lean-
ing against the wall, the cruising patrol car. It is a way of
life, and it is a way of looking at the future, or perhaps
looking away from it.

Probably no writer's historical reputation is based so solidly
on his writing about slums as is that of Jacob Riis, who was
a newspaperman in New York. His gripping and angry writing
about slum conditions had a profound impact on public policy
for many years. In 1890 he wrote a book called *How the
Other Half Lives*. Of New York's tenement slums he said:

In the tenements all the influences make for evil; because they are the hot beds of the epidemics that carry death to rich and poor alike; the nurseries of pauperism and crime that fill our jails and police courts; that throw off a scum of forty thousand human wrecks to the island asylums and workhouses year by year; that turned out in the last eight years a round half million beggars to prey upon our charities; that maintain a standing army of ten thousand tramps with all that implies; because, above all, they touch the family life with deadly moral contagion. This is their worst crime, inseparable from the system. That we have to own it the child of our own wrong does not excuse it, even though it gives it claim upon our utmost patience and tenderest charity. What are you going to do about it? is the question of today.[4]

Probably the introduction of many literate people to poverty, crime, all kinds of sinfulness, and the slums comes through *Oliver Twist.* Some of the allusions are out of date but the mood of a London slum a century and a quarter ago was not unlike that of our slums today.

The street was very narrow and muddy, and the air was impregnated with filthy odours. There were a good many small shops; but the only stock in trade appeared to be heaps of children, who, even at that time of night, were crawling in and out at the doors, or screaming from the inside. The sole places that seemed to prosper amid the general blight of the place, were the public houses; and in them, the lowest orders of Irish were wrangling with might and main. Covered ways and yards, which here and there diverged from the main street, disclosed little knots of houses, where drunken men and women were positively wallowing in filth; and from several of the doorways, great ill-looking fellows were cautiously emerging, bound, to all appearance, on no very well disposed or harmless errands.[5]

Studies and definitions

As the footnotes and bibliography of this book show, today's concern with the slums has antecedents stretching over many years and represented by many pounds of paper—and words fully as weighty. There have been commissions and committees and individual scholars who have described and analyzed and prescribed. Some of these have been responsible for important changes and improvements, while some have made little impact. What some said is as valid today as when it was published. Some contributed to the confusion or to misguided action. Some made positive contributions, but, now it is clear, said too little or were skewed by some lack of perspective. James Ford's study in the mid-nineteen-thirties was one of the last types.

Not many studies can be considered monumental, but Ford's is. It was a thoroughgoing examination of the slums of New York. He started by reviewing the way slums had been defined over the years. Then he said:

> The fundamental difficulty with all of the above definitions is that they say too much. There is, moreover, too much emphasis, often mistaken, upon local peculiarities and upon factors social rather than physical. The slum tends to be defined in terms of more or less accurately observed consequences. To conform with contemporary usage, the emphasis instead should be upon conditions of structure, age, and upkeep.
>
> We may, therefore, better define a blighted district as any area in which the large majority of buildings, whether commercial, industrial, or residential, are old, and in which fundamental repairs are no longer being made.
>
> Any area of deteriorated housing in which there is poor

upkeep of houses and premises is a blighted district and a potential slum.

Any area of old, neglected, and deteriorated housing or of new markedly substandard housing is a slum as soon as it becomes insanitary or otherwise injurious to its occupants.

The slum is thus characterized by age, neglect, and low standards or practices in sanitation.[6]

Many of the older definitions did say too much, in the sense that they generalized too broadly from the particular characteristics of a slum in one city. Ford's error, however, was more serious in the long run. He didn't say enough. He explicitly pulled back from the social and economic factors which are so profound in their influence and which must be addressed if change is to be accomplished.

Ford's summary definition of a slum was: "The slum is a residential area in which the housing is so deteriorated, so substandard, or so unwholesome as to be a menace to the health, safety, morality, or welfare of the occupants." This makes housing too dominant as the *cause* of slum conditions.

In 1931 a group of leaders who had been brought together to consider housing problems expressed themselves in these strong words.

When we speak of a slum the picture that comes to mind is a mass of more or less nondescript individual houses, tenements, stables, dilapidated shops; an absence of paint, accumulation of dirt, tin cans and rubbish. The picture is scented with a dank, damp, moldy odor, intermingled with the smell of decaying matter. We think of the slum as the abode of half-starved, filthily clothed children, of diseased and crippled individuals; a place of poverty, wretchedness, ignorance and vice. We think of it as a recession from the normal standards of a sound society . . . The slum is a distinctive area of disintegration and disorganization. It is, however, not merely the decaying and dilapidated houses, the filthy alleys and streets, nor the number of uncared for children and poverty-stricken adults which make up the slum. The slum is more than an economic condition. It is a social phenomenon in which the attitudes, ideas, ideals and practices play an important part.[7]

This begins to get closer to verity. It could as well have been written today. Unfortunately this group concluded with recommendations restricted to housing and thus did not fulfill the promise of the broad view it had taken in defining the problem.

In 1958 the New York State Division of Housing published a pamphlet called *A Primer About Slums*.[8] The cover said: *"Slum* is an ugly name for a place in which to live. It is the final phase of a neighborhood sickness that attacks our towns and cities." That is perfectly accurate as far as it goes, but, like Ford, it doesn't go far enough. The sickness is more than a neighborhood sickness and the cure must be sought beyond the neighborhood. The neighborhood is just part of the story. Later, this same pamphlet, which does quite a good job of interpreting urban renewal in a simple way, goes on to present the cure. Here it falls into common error by presenting the cure as seen by just one set of doctors—the urban renewal administrators. Now, even so soon after that pamphlet was published, very few urban renewal administrators would restrict themselves to physical renewal prescriptions and claim that thereby slums "may be cured and future growth prevented."

Three theories

Herbert Gans, a sociologist, in *The Urban Villagers* [9] studies Italians in the West End of Boston before the area was obliterated for urban renewal. He says there are two types of low-rent neighborhoods, the "entry area" and the area populated by social rejects. In the entry area newcomers to the city find their first places to live. Here they try to adapt their "non-urban institutions and cultures to the urban milieu." This is the "urban village." (Harry Barnes, in his 1931 book, *The Slum*,[10] said: "Slum dwellers take the habits formed in their old homes to the new area they enter, and their advent hastens its downward process.")

In the second type of low rent neighborhood, those who haven't succeeded and aren't going to are predominant. This is the "urban jungle." (Harry Bredemeier calls this the "jungle alms house.") In real life these types overlap and the distinctions are never crystal clear, but there are distinctions.

A theory of slums has been put forward by Charles Stokes [11] of the University of Bridgeport. Stokes divides slums into the "slums of hope" and the "slums of despair." The slum of hope is a way station. One person or family may stay there a fairly long time, but there is a feeling of transition in it. The people there are going to get out, they are on their way somewhere. These people are not yet participating fully in the economic and social life of the city, but there is reason to believe, and they feel, that some day they will.

The slum of despair is another story. This is the end of the line and there is nowhere to go from here. Again, the crucial element is that the inhabitants of such an area feel that way about it themselves. They have given up.

The *Barrio de los Pobres* (District of the Poor) of Guayaquil, Ecuador, appears hopeless. Living here must be none but the beaten and degraded. Nevertheless, this is not so. Ecuador, like other Latin American countries, has had a rapid rate of migration to the cities since World War II. People flood into the city and find or build shanties huddled next to thousands of huts just like them. Many of these are slums of hope, however, since the people have come to the city looking for a better life. The *Barrio de los Pobres* is inhabited by strangers who hope to rise and who see themselves held back by no insurmountable barriers.

Boston's South End, in contrast, is a slum of despair. On casual first impression it has an air of rundown gentility. The second impression is more real and lasting. It is, in fact, an area where the social residue lives: the old, poor, once wealthy, cast-off Bostonians; shady characters; prostitutes. Stokes sees the barriers to movement upward and outward as largely subjective. It is unlikely that most of the inhabitants of this type of slum will ever leave, but movement into the area is steady.

Within his two major divisions, slums of hope and despair (the residents of which could also be called "employable" and "unemployable"), Stokes makes another distinction. Within the slum of hope are newcomers to the city who feel that they are going to have a better place. Many of these are not going to succeed, however. Most are members of a minority group whose identification tag, skin color, is not easily erased. Too many will end in despair.

Stokes has added something useful by his way of looking at slums. He is not the first man to see the main outlines this way. Michael Harrington [12] says very much the same thing in referring to the fact that slums used to be a way station for hope but now house failures from the old waves of immigration, plus poor people of racial minorities who arrive in the slums when the economic opportunities that existed for the earlier immigrants simply are not there any more.

John R. Seeley [13] takes another tack and raises some fundamental questions about what the slum is and if it ever can or should be "extirpated." He points out that no one action is going to do away with the slum problem because the slum is many things. He also states that a change in the level of living alone, as for example the doubling of all real incomes, would not remove the problem. The slum is not just a dumping ground nor just a way station into the city. It also is a provider of goods and services that are demanded by the non-slum population, such as call girls, gambling, and crime connections. In this respect it performs a permanent function in the urban complex. This fact makes it even more difficult to change.

Like Stokes, Seeley divides slums into four basic types. There is an underlying harmony between the views of these two writers, but each has a somewhat different perspective. To Seeley, the slum population is characterized by two major differences: the difference between necessity and opportunity, and the difference between permanence and change. For some, the slum represents a set of opportunities not available as easily or at all elsewhere. For others, the slum represents a set of necessities to which, despite their wants, they have been reduced.

Thus, he sees four major types of slum dweller: the permanent necessitarians. the temporary necessitarians, the permanent opportunists, and the temporary opportunists. Among the permanent necessitarians are the indolent, the "adjusted" poor, and the social outcasts. Among the temporary necessitarians are the respectable poor, the "trapped." The permanent opportunists are fugitives, unfindables, prostitutes, and the "sporting crowd." The temporary opportunists are beginners, climbers, and "entrepreneurs."

The "feel" of a slum is as important as any other single thing about it. This refers to the feel when a nonresident is in a slum, or the feel of things when one lives in a slum. The attitude of the slum dweller toward the slum itself, toward the city of which the slum is a part, toward his own chances of getting out, toward the people who control things, toward the "system"—this is the element which as much as anything else will determine whether or not it is possible to "do something" about slums. This is what makes slums a human problem rather than a problem of finance and real estate. This is what made a real estate man in Oakland, California, say that the problem is not how to take the people out of the slums, but how to take the slums out of the people.

True as all this is, however, a rational approach demands that the problem be broken down into its component parts. Needed is a delicate process of analysis and synthesis. It is easy to lean too heavily in one direction or another, and thus to achieve a partial view. If we rest our case by saying the slum is a human problem and therefore people must be changed, we are not likely to get very far in making a difference. This serves for the ringing challenge from the podium, but then the listeners are left without much of a clue about what has to be changed or how.

On the other hand, we can break the problem into so many

parts that we fail to see all of them or how they fit together. It is like working in a laboratory, at a big table with a microscope. Having broken up the specimen for examination, we may so scatter the pieces we wish to examine that we forget to look at some of them. If this happens, our conclusion will be based on partial evidence and thus be, if not useless, not very helpful. The trouble is, a lot of money and human effort gets expended on the basis of such partial conclusions. We then wake up a few years later to the fact that the supposed solutions we grasped at earlier have made little dent on the problem.

CHAPTER II

The Elements
of the Slum
Problem Today

IT IS NOW TIME to take a look at the separate but connected elements of the slum problem. Let us hope the pieces are not scattered too widely over the laboratory table. Each of the slum elements has a negative character, a character that makes the community at large, or at least the community leadership, regard it as a "problem." Specific types of policy or action could be, and are, suggested to cope with each of these elements. The elements are all sufficiently discrete that they tend to define the function of individual community institutions. There is in every large community an agency or department to "take care" of each of these elements. The question is whether or not the elements can be dealt with separately. Since this is not a detective story it is fair to reveal the answer: they cannot. There are specific remedies that must be organized and aimed at specific problems. Food is the remedy for hunger; water is the remedy for fire; money, for poverty;

abstinence, for alcoholism; whiteness, for being Negro. But it is obvious from the absurdity of this listing that remedies thus narrowly conceived are inadequate. They are limited by the fact that they are aimed at symptoms and not causes, and they imbue their target problems with an insulation that they do not, in real life, have.

What this leads to, of course, is the truism that a double process must take place: identifying and isolating the problem phenomenon along with developing specific remedies for it; and linking the particular phenomenon and the proposed remedies to others in the same universe and to the total setting. This is the ecology of cause and cure.

The identifiable features of the slum problem are these:

Poverty, absolute or relative. It may hurt more if it's relative, that is if you are relatively poor in the midst of affluence.

Run-down housing. The degree of dilapidation is not always uniform throughout a slum. A reservation also should be entered here with reference to public housing. Sometimes public housing seems slum-like even though the buildings themselves are new.

Crowding. High density per square mile or per block or census tract doesn't necessarily mean a slum. Some high rent areas have high density, according to a given ground measurement. They do not have high occupancy per room, as does a slum.

Concentration of lower class people. By all measures of social class—occupation, level of education, location of residence, community reputation, style of life, standard of living, membership in organizations, use of leisure—the slums are full of lower class people. These people are low according to the various measures by which we locate people in our society and decide whether or not we want our children to associate with them.

Racial concentration. Slums of the inner city are increasingly populated by dark-skinned people (Negroes primarily, but also Puerto Ricans and Mexicans, depending on the part of the country). The population is becoming more and more homogeneous. This feature is euphemistically called the "changing composition of the inner city."

Concentration of people of low educational achievement, low skill, and cultural limitations. Such characteristics make it very difficult for people to find their niches in an increasingly technological economy.

Many welfare cases. A flow chart showing where checks for unemployment compensation, aid to dependent children, old age assistance, and other kinds of relief go would have heavy black lines converging on the slums.

Internal mobility. More people in the slums move about to more places more frequently than do people who live in other places. These moves, in the main, are made within the slum area, or from one slum to another, or to a gray area.

Crime. More crimes are committed by adults and by juveniles in slums. This is so be the measure number of arrests, or sample studies of confidentially reported crimes which may or may not involve arrest. Certain types of crime, of course, such as bank robberies, jewel thefts, and corporate embezzlement, are not typical of the slums.

Health problems. More people in the slums are physically and mentally ill. Slum dwellers do not live as long as non-slum dwellers.

Broken families. One out of four American families is broken by divorce. In the slums this rate runs higher. Many broken families in the slums would more properly be called "partial" families since the parents were never legally united in the first place. There are more children born out of wedlock in the slums than elsewhere. The rate is higher among Negroes than among whites.

Relocation problems. This term came into the language at the end of World War II, deriving from the physical urban renewal programs undertaken since then. These programs are sometimes called "Negro removal programs," or "slum dweller removal programs," since many residents of slums have had to move somewhere else to make way for new building. This has been a slum problem because much urban renewal has had the double objective of clearing slums and replacing them with better revenue-producing property such as business buildings or higher rent apartment buildings. Highway construction has also been a big slum remover.

Inadequate community services. Street repair, policing, garbage collection, building inspection, schooling, health service, and welfare services are never adequate in the slums.

Skid row. Skid row is a special kind of slum. It collects more than just drunks. Every city has one.

Isolation and alienation. This is probably one of the most important things about a slum, or rather, about the people in it. They tend to be isolated from many things that make for the integration of people in a dynamic, mutually reinforcing social and economic system. Some are isolated. Some are alienated, which means they are not merely separate from, but also against.

Dirt. Slums are dirtier than other places. This is one of the things that can readily be seen even when passing through.

Fire hazards. There are more fires, more property damage,

more loss of life or injury from fires in the slums than in other parts of the city or in the suburbs.

Language problems. The language of America is good English. Many residents of slums whose mother tongue is Spanish can hardly speak English. In the old days, there were more pockets of Hungarian, Polish, Yiddish, German, Italian, and Lithuanian speaking people than there are now. The language problem also applies to many people whose mother tongue is English, such as southern Negroes and whites from the Appalachians or the Ozarks. They speak a kind of English, but not the kind that helps them move up in the world.

The slum atmosphere. This is what all the above elements add up to. It is more than the sum of its parts, and itself becomes a separate element, a qualitative factor of influence in the lives of slum dwellers.

Some of these elements deserve elaboration.

Poverty

It has come as a surprise to many people that there is still so much poverty in America, and that it still has to be regarded as a problem. John Kenneth Galbraith invented the descriptive term, affluent society. This is the way we think of America, and with good reason. When one looks at our position relative to the rest of the world, we are definitely affluent. The acres and acres of new homes in the areas surrounding the big cities, and the small ones, too, certainly indicate that a lot of people are able to earn the down payment and fees necessary to buy a home. The great new office buildings and apartments in the city itself must have somebody to rent them or they wouldn't be built. It is not possible to see very many people wandering around in shabby clothes, in most places. The sales of all kinds of consumer goods—cars, television sets, jewelry, household appliances—mean there are consumers buying things. Where is the poverty? It is in the urban and rural slums. It is in the large depressed areas of the Southern Appalachians and Northern Minnesota and in the depressed areas of the cities—big, middlesized, and small.

In 1958, writing about the affluent society, Galbraith said: "Poverty does survive. In the United States the survival of poverty is remarkable. We ignore it because we share with all societies at all times the capacity for not seeing what we do not wish to see." [1]

In 1963, Galbraith, engaged in an assignment from President John Kennedy to help plan a national anti-poverty strategy, stated that ever since *The Affluent Society* had appeared he had been accused (by those who never read the book carefully) of thinking there were no more poor in the United States. In a speech that received national attention Galbraith emphasized that there are still plenty of poor and that "the problem of poverty in the United States is the problem of people who for reasons of location, education, health, environment in youth, or mental deficiency, or who because of racial discrimination are not able to participate effectively—or at all —in the economic life of the nation. Being barred from participation they are denied the income that accrues to participants. So they live in privation." [2]

The facts of poverty are these: Twenty per cent of all Americans live in poverty; another 20 per cent live at a level that can reasonably be called deprived. These are statements not easily challenged. Different sources may interpret "poverty" or an "adequate standard of living" somewhat differently, but the import is constant in all responsible studies.

In 1960 over 77 million people in the United States lived in poverty or deprivation. Over 34 million people in 10.5 million families had incomes of less than $4,000 in that year, and 4 million unattached individuals earned less than $2,000. This adds up to 38 million people, or about one-fifth of the total population.

If "deprivation" is taken to mean family income between $4,000 and $6,000 and unattached individual income between $2,000 and $3,000, 37 million people in 10.3 million families and 2 million unattached individuals were in this category. This represents another one-fifth of the total population.

Thus, we reach the broad conclusion that two-fifths of the population live in poverty or deprivation.[3] This has a familiar ring to those who remember the famous "One-third of a nation is ill-fed, ill-clothed, and ill-housed."

President Johnson's Economic Report to Congress on January 20, 1964, said that 35 million men, women, and children live without hope, below minimum standards of decency. Their per capita income in 1962 was only $590 as against $1,900 per capita for the nation as a whole.

A study done by Robert J. Lampman for the United States Congress, in 1959,[4] reported that for 1957 there were 32.2 million low income persons. This was 19.1 per cent of the total population. As a standard of measurement, Lampman used an "income equivalent to that of a member of a four-person family with total money income of not more than $2,500 in 1957 dollars." For an unattached individual, this meant $1,157 and for a family of six, $3,236. In order to avoid charges of gilding the lily, Lampman pointed out that this standard was well below the Bureau of Labor Statistics 1957 level of $4,000 necessary for an adequate standard of living.

The National Policy Committee on Pockets of Poverty, on March 5, 1964, released a report entitled *Poverty in America.* This report stressed the fact that poverty is not evenly spread through the population, but concentrated in groups with "poverty linked characteristics." Although one of eight families in the general population had income below $2,000 in 1960, this rose to one in three among the "poverty linked" families: non-white, female head, over 65, rural-farm, less than eight years schooling, part-time work experience.

If poverty is defined as embracing families with income of less than $4,500, more than two out of three of these families are poor. In families with two or more of these characteristics, three out of four of them are poor.

This committee accepts the validity of three levels of poverty: minimum subsistence ($2,500 per year for family of four); minimum adequacy ($3,500); minimum comfort ($5,500). In 1960, 20 million people were in families below the minimum subsistence level; 46 million were below minimum adequacy; 70 million fell below minimum comfort.

Michael Harrington [5] says there are between 40 and 50 million poor people in America. He referred to the AFL-CIO report that 41.5 million people, 24 per cent of the population, had demonstrably substandard incomes. That meant that in 1958, 36 million people lived in families of two or more persons with incomes of less than $3,000. Another 5.5 million individuals had incomes of less than $1,500.

Harrington felt that Lampman's case was understated, because the Bureau of Labor Statistics had revised its basis for determining an adequate standard after his report was issued. The new adequate family budget for four people in the city ranged from $5,370 in Houston to $6,567 in Chicago. This level is called "modest but adequate" and below the average enjoyed by American families. It is far from gracious living.

Senator Eugene J. McCarthy [6] took the measure of poverty by quoting the United States Statistical Abstract for 1960: 8 million families had incomes under $2,500 and another 7 million between $2,500 and $4,000. He pointed out that in 1958, 14.3 per cent of all families and unattached individuals had incomes less than $2,000; 10 per cent were between $2,000 and $3,000; 12 per cent, between $3,000 and $4,000. In sum, 36.3 per cent were below $4,000. Seven million families were receiving public assistance in 1960.

The International Brotherhood of Teamsters, in June, 1962, released information about low income in New York.[7] Their study showed that 49 per cent of the families in the New York metropolitan area had incomes below the level established by the Bureau of Labor Statistics as "modest but adequate." For New York in 1959, this was $5,970 for a family of four. The Teamster release said, "One out of every two New York families in the metropolitan area lives at a level of denial or deprivation or degradation." While the over-all percentage of the population at that level was 49, it was considerably higher, 70.8 per cent, for Negro and Puerto Rican families.

In New York City, Mayor Wagner released a report ("Dimensions of Poverty in New York City," Office of the City Administrator, March 23, 1964) pointing out that 18 per cent of the city's population had incomes below $3,000 per year (478,000 individuals, 317,000 families). Twenty-seven per cent had incomes below $4,000. Basing his conclusions on a sliding-scale definition of poverty, the Mayor stated that one in every five New Yorkers lives at the poverty level. Fifty-two per cent of these are white (85 per cent of the total population is white). Twenty-nine per cent are non-white (mostly Negro) and 19 per cent are Puerto Rican.

The Detroit Area Study [8] in 1957 reported that for the period 1951 through 1955 the proportion of families in Detroit receiving less than $3,000 never was under 14 per cent. In 1955, 41 per cent of the families had incomes of less than $5,000.

In the San Francisco Bay Area in 1959 among 865,588 families, 25.4 per cent had median income below $5,000, and 11.5 per cent were below $3,000. Among Negro families, 46.6 per cent were below $5,000 and 22.4 per cent below $3,000, as compared with 23.2 per cent below $5,000 and 10.4 per cent below $3,000 among whites.

The problem of statisticians and researchers and social workers has always been to put flesh and blood on data such as these. Think of $6,000 as an annual income for a family of four. (Remember, about 40 per cent of our population has only this much money or less.) One round trip air fare, tourist class, New York to California, costs about $300. One small sailboat costs $3,000. One year of college costs $3,000. One modest car costs $2,500. One summer at camp costs $700. One new furnace costs $1,000. Not many of the 40 per cent are going to spend their money on these things, which middle class families do not think out of order at all.

This means that very many American families simply are not going to be able to spend money on a lot of things that add breadth and depth to life. For instance, the list above notes that a year of college costs $3,000. Patricia Sexton, in *Education and Income,*[9] pointed out that college attendance varies almost exactly with family income. A study in a large midwestern city showed that only about 23 per cent of the graduating high school students whose families had incomes of $5,000 or below requested credit transcripts in order to apply for college admission. In the $5,000-$6,000 income bracket, 34 per cent requested transcripts. The percentage for the $9,000 and over bracket was 81 per cent.

It would not be correct to think of families with incomes around the $5,000 or $6,000 level as living in utter privation and misery. In general, the mood in this group is that income is not very much. Pennies have to be pinched. It just is not possible to think of spending for many extras. Such a family is not going to be a heavy customer in an expanding economy. Such a family is not going to contribute frequently to the highly-educated manpower that will be more and more needed in our cybernating society.

Down around the $4,000 and below family income level is real, indisputable poverty. At this level it is possible to use words like misery, defeat, terror, and chaos. This point doesn't need to be stressed. It just needs to be thought about by decision makers who are concerned about our society's general health.

The poor contribute very little in terms of stimulation for economic growth, intellectual leadership, scientific or cultural creativity, and just plain good citizenship. And yet there is no evidence that such people, as a group, inherently have less to offer than any other group. The problem is that it is difficult for human productivity to sprout from the barren soil of poverty.

The slum is the locus of poverty, and poverty is one of the

potent forces that maintains the vicious circle and makes it so difficult for people to break out. A simple redistribution of income is not enough to eliminate poverty permanently, but some moves in that direction are certainly relevant. For the first time in the history of the human race, it is possible to think in terms of the *elimination* of poverty at least in one country. In the United States the resources are available. Just from a monetary point of view, it would cost something like 10 billion dollars per year to eliminate poverty. This represents 2 per cent of the gross national product, less than 10 per cent of current tax revenues, and one-fifth of the cost of national defense.[10]

There has been more poverty and deprivation in the United States than most people think. Although, as the references here show, some serious voices have been calling attention to this anomaly during the past several years, it was not raised to its proper place on the agenda of public policy until President Johnson announced the "war on poverty" and appointed Sargent Shriver to head the program.

Run-down housing

Slum housing includes both buildings that have deteriorated from their original livable state and buildings that never were fit for human habitation. There are not so many of the latter any more in the cities. There are plenty in the rural slums, particularly in the South. This type of building was typified by the "old law tenement" of New York (there are still over 50,000 of them), which has inside rooms with no ventilation at all, minimal sanitary facilities, little light, and is constructed of combustible materials throughout.

Today in the big cities most of the buildings in the slums

once were fairly decent, and could be made so again. In 1960, there were 3,684,000 urban slum housing units.[11] Of these, 1,173,000 were "dilapidated urban units" by the standard definition used in the 1960 census.

The remaining 2,511,000 were urban housing units lacking some or all plumbing facilities. In this urban slum housing, at least 12.5 million people lived. This was calculated on the basis of 3.36 persons per household, the average for the United States. Urban households tend to be somewhat smaller than the general average, but urban slum households tend to be larger than the general urban average. Therefore, this is a reasonable basis for estimating the number of people living in slums. The figure has to be estimated because it was not counted, as such, in the 1960 census. Slum dwellings in one or another degree of fitness for human habitation are defined for the purposes of census taking as follows: [12]

Dilapidated housing does not provide safe and adequate shelter. It has one or more critical defects; or has a combination of intermediate defects in sufficient number to require extensive repair or rebuilding; or is of inadequate original construction. Critical defects result from continued neglect or lack of repair or indicate serious damage to the structure. Examples of critical defects include: holes, open cracks or missing materials over a large area of the floors, walls, roof, or other parts of the structure; sagging floors, walls or roof; damage by storm or fire. Inadequate original construction includes structures built of makeshift materials and inadequately converted cellars, sheds, or garages not originally intended as living quarters.

Dilapidated units are shown in two classes. Those with private toilet and bath and hot water and those with flush toilet exclusive use; bathtub or shower, exclusive use; and hot and cold piped water within the structure. All other dilapidated units are included in the category "lacking hot water, private toilet, or bath."

Deteriorating housing needs more repair than would be provided in the course of regular maintenance. It has one or more defects of an intermediate nature that must be corrected if the unit is to continue to provide safe and adequate shelter. Examples of intermediate defects include: shaky or unsafe porch or steps; holes, open cracks, or missing materials over a small area of the floors, walls, or roof; rotted window sills or frames; deep wear on floors, stairs, or door sills; broken or loose stair treads or missing balusters. Such defects indicate neglect which leads to serious deterioration or damage if not corrected.

Not all definitions of slum dwellings are the same. The Committee on Economic Progress included in its estimate of about 5 million slum dwellings in metropolitan areas those dwelling units which were considered to be "seriously deficient." These house about 17 million people. There were another 4.5 million of these dwellings in rural areas. A further 6.2 million in both urban and rural areas "needed repair and alterations, including modernization, beyond ordinary maintenance requirements." Of the 9.5 million seriously deficient units, 5.2 million were so bad as to require replacement. They could not be brought up to standard by repair. About half of them were in urban slums.

One might assume that anyone who is bothering to read a book like this must be well acquainted with what a slum dwelling looks, smells, and feels like. This is not a safe assumption. Very few people who do not live there or whose jobs do not take them there ever do more than drive through the slums. Even fewer get inside slum buildings. Public welfare investigators go there, firemen go inside, so do policemen and building inspectors (although the last probably not nearly enough). A few dedicated ministers and priests, and bill collectors and politicians-on-the-make may go sometimes. But even the supervisors of these people do not get to the slums often. In the old days they may have, but when their jobs do not require them to make the rounds any more they naturally have no great urge to go back and see how things are.

Some less scientific and precise descriptions of slum dwellings perhaps give a stronger impression of reality. In 1919, Dr. John Robertson, in his book *Housing and Public Health*,[13] said, "A town slum dwelling may be structurally good, and yet, from its darkened surroundings, its absence of free air supply, its soot-laden atmosphere, and its filthy environment, it may be one of the most unwholesome dwellings." That was said over forty years ago, but it still rings true.

B. S. Townroe, in 1928, in *The Slum Problem*,[14] spoke of slum dwellings this way: "windows dirty, broken and patched with white or brown paper; curtains dirty and frayed, and blinds half drawn and often hanging at an angle. The street doors are usually open, showing bare passages and stairs lacking bannisters, while the door jambs are generally brown with dirt, and rubbed shiny by the coats of the leisured class, whose habit is to lean up against them."

Harvey Zorbaugh, in 1929, in his book about Chicago, *The Gold Coast and the Slum*,[15] had this to say: "These rooms are stove heated, and wood is sold on the streets in bundles, and coal in small sacks. The majority of houses, back toward the river, are of wood, and not a few have windows broken out. Smoke, the odor from the gas works, and the smell of dirty alleys is in the air. Both rooms and lots are overcrowded."

Jacob Riis wrote with real fire about slums and tenements. This is what he saw.

Today (1890) what is a tenement? The law defines it as a house "Occupied by three or more families, living independently and doing their cooking on the premises; or by more than two families on a floor, so living and cooking, and having a common right in the halls, stairways, yards, etc." That is the legal meaning. In its narrower sense the typical tenement was thus described when last arraigned before the bar of public justice: "It is generally a brick building from four to six stories high on the street, frequently with stores on the first floor which, when used for the sale of liquor, has a side opening for the benefit of the inmates and to evade the Sunday law; four families occupy each floor, and a set of rooms consists of one or two dark closets, used as bedrooms, with a living room twelve feet by ten. The staircase is too often a dark well in the centre of the house, and no direct through ventilation is possible, each family being separated from the other by partitions. The picture is nearly as true today as ten years ago, and will be for a long time to come. The dim light admitted by the air shaft shines upon greater crowds than ever. Tenements are still "good property" and the poverty of the poor man his destruction. A barrack downtown where he *has* to live because he is poor brings in a third more rent than a decent house in Harlem. The statement once made a sensation that between seventy and eighty children had been found in one tenement.

Spite of brown stone trimmings, plate glass and mosaic vestibule floors, the water does not rise in summer to the second story, while the beer flows unchecked to the all night picnics on the roof. The saloon with the side door and the landlord divide the prosperity of the place between them and the tenant, in sullen submission, foots the bills." [16]

Housing improved in the decade between 1950 and 1960. In 1950, 17 million housing units were dilapidated. This was 37 per cent of the total housing stock, urban and rural. In 1960, the figure was 10.6 million units dilapidated or lacking in one or more plumbing facilities. This was 18 per cent of the total housing stock. The southeastern area of the country, with three tenths of the total housing, had half of the dilapidated housing.

There was also less overcrowding. In 1940, 20 per cent of all housing units had 1.01 or more persons per room. In 1950, this was 16 per cent and in 1960, 12 per cent.

Crowding

High densities are characteristic of slums. But high densities don't necessarily mean an area is a slum. There are some very expensive living zones in most of the big cities that have high densities.

Densities in slum areas are tending gradually to decrease. Therefore, like all the other features of slums, high density must be looked at in connection with other factors, in order that its true significance in relation to slum conditions be understood. There are some articulate voices in America now arguing strongly for the preservation and recreation of high densities.

In a slum, high density is the result of the need to find cheap housing. Here, density means crowding too many people into buildings that are in neighborhoods with too many such overcrowded buildings and without proper services for cleaning, maintenance, and repair.

High density among wealthier people may be desirable in

terms of generating social relationships, variety in life, interest and excitement deriving from many people and activities, and a sense of society. Some of these same elements are no doubt present in the slum, but the added elements of lack of privacy, noise, nuisance, and violence are more likely to be present and to be geometrically enhanced by the neighborhood density.

We still have a way to go in reducing densities and over-crowding in slum areas. Michael Harrington dramatized this by pointing out that if the densities of some of Harlem's worst blocks obtained in the rest of New York City, the entire population of the United States could fit into three of New York's boroughs.

Lower class people

All lower class people do not live in the slums, but practically all the people who live in the slums are lower class or at the lower end of a status-ranking continuum.

In America any discussion of social class, or social stratification, is almost bound to be affected by emotionalism and mythology. Many have liked to pretend that we have a classless society. The Marxists claim that one of the inherent features of capitalist society is that it is built in layers, that these layers are determined solely by the economic system, and that if you are in the bottom layer that is where you will stay until the revolution. They also say that it is the essential function of the people in the top layers to exploit people in the lower layers.

The traditional American response to this is that while it is true that some people are better off than others, this is because of their initiative, drive, and capacity, and that everybody has an equal chance to rise because ours is an open society. We do not block people from rising by artificial social categories such as royalty, serfdom, slavery, or caste. It is this openness that makes our society and economy dynamic and growing, since the competition for material things and for higher position energizes us and brings out the best of our productive capacities.

Neither of these points of view is wholly true or wholly false. History has shown that those societies that say they are now Marxist are in fact still built like layer cakes. The layers may be identified by different characteristics from those in capitalist societies, but they are undeniably there. This is one of the points, if not the main point, of *The New Class,* by Milovan Djilas of Yugoslavia.[17]

On the other hand, a dispassionate look at our own society clearly reveals that we do have social classes in America and even some touches of caste. Because this is one of the important aspects of the formation and perpetuation of slums, it is worth spending some time on here.

Walter Miller estimates that between 40 per cent and 60 per cent of the total population of the United States "share or are significantly influenced by the major outlines of the lower class cultural system," [18] with 15 per cent being the "hard core" lower class group (25,000,000). This system is defined by a series of "focal concerns": *trouble*—getting into and staying out of trouble; *toughness*—physical prowess, masculinity, endurance, strength; *smartness*—outsmarting the other guy, duping the teacher, avoiding being duped by others; *excitement*—the search for thrills and stimulation, goading the authorities, participating in a rumble; *fate*—Lady Luck as reigning goddess and shaper of destiny; *autonomy*—"no one is going to boss me," overt expression of disdain and dislike for external control.

S. M. Miller believes that low paid, unskilled, irregular employment is essentially what defines the lower class. Jay Cohen emphasizes an unstable family pattern and other factors of "personal" instability.

Herbert Gans, in *The Urban Villagers,* identified a number of indicators of lower class status when he studied the West End of Boston: the display and defense of masculinity; the search for excitement; the central role of the peer group; the subordinate role of children; a lack of interest in children as individuals; freedom permitted for boys as against a tendency to keep girls at home; the extended family; rather separate social lives of men and women; concrete and anecdotal conversation; detachment from the job; concern with job security; negative view of white collar workers and bosses; a lack of trust in the outside world; a personalization of government ("the lady at the Welfare"); antagonism toward law and government.

These are the guides by which it is possible to assign someone to a lower social class position. These class lines cut across religious and ethnic groups and are relevant to an understanding of the way of life of the people in them. Gans's final definition is that "classes are strata-with-subcultures that grow out of the structure of the national economy and society."

Gans also distinguishes between the working class and the lower class. Working class people are semi-skilled and skilled blue collar workers who hold steady jobs and thus are able to live under stable, if not affluent, conditions. "Their ways of life differ in many respects from those of the middle class; for example in the greater role of relatives in sociability and mutual aid, in the lesser concern for self improvement and education, and in their lack of interest in the good address, high culture, and the kinds of status that are important to middle class people." He points out that these are significant differences but they are not *problem-producing* differences; they are not pathological, since rates of crime, mental illness, and other social ills are not significantly higher for the working class than for the middle class.

The lower class, on the other hand, does have characteristic differences that produce problems. Lack of stability in jobs, unemployment, and social and emotional instability related to occupational instability are some of them.

Leonard Reissman says: "classes do exist even though individuals are not chained to these social positions with unequivocal finality. This does not imply that everyone—or even a majority—reaches the level of economic comfort, social recognition, or authority that he wants or perhaps even deserves. American society appears to be at a stage that is somewhat short of either extreme, even though we would like to believe in the notion of an open class society that is fair and impartial." [19]

Is there in America a process of stratifying individuals or groups in terms of their differential access to power and its sources, whether economic, political, or prestige? The answer is yes. Frank Riessman gives this "portrait of the underprivileged":

He is traditional, "old fashioned" in many ways, patriarchal (except a major section of the Negro subculture), superstitious, somewhat religious, though not so religious as his wife. He reads ineffectively, is poorly informed in many areas, and is often suggestible, although interestingly enough, he is frequently suspicious of "talk" and "newfangled ideas."

He is confused and without opinion in many areas but has strong conviction in others such as morality, punishment, custom, diet, traditional education, the role of women, and intellectuals. He frequently feels alienated and left out of society and thus believes in the corruptness of leaders and is antagonistic toward "big shots." He is not individualistic, introspective, moderate. He holds the world, rather than himself responsible for his ills. He desires to "get by" rather than to "get ahead." He does not want to become a foreman because of the economic insecurity resulting from loss of job seniority. He is not class-conscious, and while he is somewhat radical on a few economic issues, he is distinctly illiberal on numerous matters, particularly civil liberties and foreign policy. He is not interested in politics, does not vote a good deal of the time, and generally belongs to few organizations. He tends to favor the underdog and his relationships to people are marked by an equalitarian outspoken informality. He is strongly anti-communist, but he does possess a number of traits that have authoritarian potential: he likes strong leaders, he is prejudiced and intolerant, he is less likely to see the need for having dissident opinions. He sets great store by his family and his personal comforts. He likes excitement—to get away from the humdrum of daily life. He is pragmatic and anti-intellectual. There is a strong emphasis on masculinity.[20]

A landmark study of social class in America was made by W. Lloyd Warner, with Marcia Meeker and Kenneth Eells.[21] Warner approached his study as an anthropologist rather than as a social theorist. He went into a town and "discovered" that it had a social class structure, through his field observations and interviews. Six classes were found: upper-upper (old aristocracy); lower-upper (aristocracy, but not old); upper-middle ("people who should be upper class"); lower-middle ("we poor folk"); upper-lower ("poor but honest folk"); lower-lower ("people just as good as anybody"). These characteristics were based on people's perception of what class they themselves were in and what classes other people were in. Warner called this the Evaluated Participation. He also used a more objective Index of Status Characteristics. This was based on occupation, source of income (whether wages, salary, or dividends), house type, and dwelling area.

J. A. Kahl, in 1957,[22] concluded that the social classes in America could be identified by six criteria: occupational prestige, style of life, interaction patterns, personal prestige, value orientations, and class consciousness.

Oscar Lewis, in his graphic description of poverty in Mexico, lists traits characteristic of what he calls the "culture of poverty," pointing out that there are remarkable similarities in lower class settlements in London, Glasgow, Paris, Harlem, and Mexico City.[23] Lewis' list does make sense, even though one can imagine he is hearing it in French, Spanish, English, or a totally unfamiliar Asiatic language:

Provincial and locally oriented
Members only partially integrated into national institutions
Marginal people even though in the heart of a big city
Low level of education and literacy
People do not belong to labor unions
People not members of a political party.
People do not participate in medical care, old-age benefits,
    maternity care, and make little use of the city's hospitals,

banks, department stores, museums, art galleries, and
airports
Unemployment and underemployment
Low wages
People unskilled
Child labor
No savings
Chronic shortage of cash
No food reserves in the home
Pawning of personal goods
Borrowing small amounts at usurious rates
Use of second-hand clothing and furniture
Crowded living quarters
Lack of privacy
Much alcoholism
Frequent resort to violence
Violence in the training of children
Wife beating
Early sex experience
Free unions or "consensual" marriage
High incidence of desertion of wives and children
Mother-centered families
Authoritarianism
Emphasis on family solidarity (an ideal rarely achieved)
Present time orientation (live for the present)
A sense of resignation and fatalism based on the realities
of the difficult real life situation
A belief in male superiority
Martyr complex among women
A high tolerance for psychological pathology of all kinds

Hatred of the police

Mistrust of government

A cynicism which gives the culture of poverty a potential for being used in political movements aimed against the existing social order

Richard Cloward, in uncomplicated language, says of the lower classes: "The typical lower class person has had less than an eighth grade education, is employed as an unskilled or service worker, and lives in a family whose income per person is less than the minimum wage." [24] Cloward places people in the "working class" if they are skilled workers, clerks, or salesmen with some high school education.

Not everyone is willing to divide things up in terms of classes or stratification. Various writers prefer to think that American society is characterized by a continuum. Among these is Art Gallaher, who found that this was true in his re-study of Plainville, U.S.A. He visited a middle-sized Missouri town ten years after it had been studied by another anthropologist, James West (the *nom de plume* of Carl Withers). The continuum people, however, don't deny that there is a top and bottom of the continuum and that this has implications for what people do, how they think, where they live, and so forth.

Some responsible thinkers worry about an oversimplification of the concepts of social class no matter how it is measured. One of these is Alfred Kahn of the Columbia University School of Social Work. In a personal communication Kahn said:

Too much of what is being said about class and its effect is based on an oversimplified model which ignores generational, ethnic, racial, regional factors and which ignores what social science has said about the class concept *per se*. Too much of the current "new programs" literature in social work and education is based on a romantic-idealized concept of coherent lower class culture to be protected and perpetuated, whereas all the reality suggests that a) for many the aspirations are in the direction of upward mobility, and b) devices offered as ways to reach "lower class culture" participants on their own terms for education, etc., have the effect of handicapping them *vis à vis* the broader opportunity structures.

This view does not deny the fact that some people are at the bottom of our society and others are at the top or in the middle ranges. This fact, whether tied to social class or to a more fluid continuum, is a prime factor in controlling what happens in the future to those people and their children.

It does not take much argument to make the point that the slums are full of low status people. The arguments will come around to other subjects, such as whether most of the people want to stay there and whether slums are dumping grounds or way stations.

Most writers accept the fact that class position or rank in the social scale depends on things like occupation, education, and income. We have also seen that some of the prime identifiers of slums are deteriorated housing, overcrowded dwelling units, and high density (in combination). The facts about a few census tracts from several large cities immediately demonstrate that the tracts measuring low in the social class indices measure high on the slum indices (Table 1).

Table 1—Clustering of Status Indicators by Census Tracts

CITY TRACT	MEDIAN FAMILY INCOME IN DOLLARS		BLUE COLLAR MALE WORKERS, IN PER CENT		HIGH SCHOOL GRADUATES AGE 25 AND OVER, IN PER CENT		NEGROES, IN PER CENT		SOUND HOUSING UNITS, IN PER CENT		HOUSING UNITS WITH MORE THAN 1.01 PERSON PER ROOM, IN PER CENT	
	Low	Medium	Low	Medium	Low	Medium	Low	Medium	Low	Medium	Low	Medium
Chicago												
#370	3731		74		14		16		83		25	
#343		7200		30		39		under 1		93		7
Detroit												
#0036	3746		70		12		20		42		17	
#0210		7264		39		40		under 1		94		3
St. Louis												
#0018-E	3729		74		17		65		47		26	
#0013		7245		63		60		under 1		99		1
Boston												
#Q0003	3793		68		28		33		54		15	
#X0003B		7203		37		57		under 1		90		5
Los Angeles												
#2031	3586		60		17		16 70*		62		45	
#1034		7202		27		56		0		99		6

* Spanish surname.

Several special studies in smaller cities show the same correlation. Charles Willie and Morton Wagenfeld of the Youth Development Center at the University of Syracuse [25] examined the census tracts of Syracuse and Onondaga County using five measures: a) the percentage of craftsmen, operatives, service workers, and laborers; b) the median school year completed by the adult population over twenty-five years of age; c) the estimated market value of owned homes; d) the gross monthly rental for tenant occupied dwellings; and e) the percentage of sound dwelling units.

A few representative census tracts are shown in Table 2.

Table 2—Representative Census Tracts

TRACT NUMBER	24 low status	22 low status	59 middle status	47 high status
a. Per cent craftsmen, operatives, laborers, etc.	53.1	42.3	29.9	10.7
b. Years of school	8.8	9.7	11.6	13.0
c. Value of owned house (dollars)	9,200	11,100	12,700	25,000+
d. Rent (dollars)	73	74	85	117
e. Per cent sound dwelling units	59.6	34.1	97.4	99.9

The New York City Youth Board [26] compiled some social problem indices for the city. Three health areas are illustrative of how indices run in packs (Table 3).

Maurice D. Van Arsdol of the Youth Studies Center of the University of Southern California made a study of Santa Monica. He pointed out that all cities are composed of contrasting neighborhood populations and that people move into neigh-

Table 3—Social Problem Indices

Index	HEALTH AREA (MANHATTAN)		
	#10	#11	#31.20
Whites	85	4212	22136
Negroes	21,953	7739	1114
Puerto Ricans	91	2817	1186
Median family income	$3,998	$4,535	$7,203
Juvenile delinquency rate (per 1000 youths age 7-20)	107.7	96.6	29.8
Aid to Dependent Children rate (per 1000 youths)	258.3	195.5	63.1
Venereal disease rate per 100,000 population	1,538.5	414.9	240
Per cent overcrowded housing			
Total	8.90	7.24	7.50
Non-white	8.90	7.25	26.90
Per cent of children in school in			
kindergarten	6.6	4.4	4.5
elementary	65.8	66.6	53.5
high school	27.6	29.0	42.0

borhoods on the basis of noneconomic values attached to residence location, as well as on the basis of ability to pay. Neighborhood populations differ in status, family organization, sex and age structure, values, and patterns of social interaction, as well as economic level. In other words, they differ in class.

Census tracts in Santa Monica were ranked according to relative power and prestige. The elements that went into this ranking were occupational status of the residents, years of schooling completed, and median rent. It was no surprise to find that the elements of the index an area high in occupational status was high in education and rent, and vice versa. The lowest ranking areas were occupied by non-whites and Spanish surname people.

There are groups of people lower in status than others

according to indices by which status can be measured. There is enough congruence among these indices so that it is correct to identify groups as "classes" as long as this is not done too rigidly. The lower class groups are found in the slums and gray areas.

One compelling reason for regarding slums as a major American problem is this fact of the concentration of low status or low class people in the slums, and the knowledge that it is very difficult to break out of the trap. How does this trap or vicious circle work? A child born in the slums or moving there is caught in a complex of destructive factors that reinforce each other. Overcoming them requires more strength than most men have.

The chances are that a slum child lives with parent or parents or adults with little education. His parents do not read much beyond the lowest level tabloid, if that. They do not converse in any meaningful sense of the word. They do not know much about the world, or even the city and its problems and opportunities. Their horizons are limited. They probably realize that education is important to getting ahead, but they do not see it as a real possibility for themselves or their kind. They do not provide a stimulus or encouragement for the child to benefit from his schooling. They probably expect the child to drop out of school before finishing high school or certainly not to go on beyond high school.

Thus the slum child has a different attitude toward school than does the middle class, suburban child. The wealthier child does not consciously think about school as a means to his later advancement, but his atmosphere is saturated with the idea that school is an important part of his life. This feeling is intensified in the higher grades when college entrance is closer and he is bombarded by frightening news from friends, parents, teachers, and mass media that colleges are hard to get into, and he had better do well in high school if he expects admittance. In his world he is expected to make it, because going to college is the thing to do.

Through this process the sights of the slum child are subtly being lowered, or at least are prevented from rising. He begins to adopt an image of himself as a person who will stop at a certain level of education and as a person who is liable to wind up on the lower rungs of the occupational ladder. He sometimes may express fanciful aspirations to be a scientist or an engineer. Deeper probing reveals that he knows this is an unrealistic expectation.

What people think of themselves is of crucial importance. It is one of the determining factors in whether or not they get out of the slums. All the conditions of slum life combine to tell a child day and night that he is not worth much.

There are other things that make us doubt that schooling in the slums will "take." Dedicated teachers devoting their lives to good teaching under the trying conditions of slum schools are the exception rather than the rule. Teaching quality is lower in the inner city than in the suburbs. Classes are more crowded. Equipment is not as good and there is not as much of it. Thus, the children who have less motivation for schooling and less support in home, neighborhood, and among their friends, and who need a little extra in the schoolroom if they are to be helped, in fact get less. The weakness or downright destructiveness of the environment outside the school is not compensated for, where compensation possibly could make a difference. Really good education, geared to the needs of children from poor backgrounds, in many cases could give these children the necessary push to break out of the vicious circle.

Talking about the effects of poor housing (housing being interpreted here very broadly to include the neighborhood surroundings as well), Alvin Schorr said:

> The following effects may spring from poor housing: a perception of one's self that leads to pessimism and passivity, stress to which the individual cannot adapt, poor health, and a state of dissatisfaction; pleasure in company but not in solitude, cynicism about people and organizations, a high degree of sexual stimulation without legitimate outlet, and difficulty in household management and child rearing; and relationships that tend to spread out in the neighborhood rather than deeply into the family. Most of these effects in turn place obstacles in the path of improving one's financial circumstances. Obstacles such as those presented by poor health or inability to train children are obvious. Those presented by having ties centered in one's neighborhood rather than in one's wife and children are less direct, but significant. Such a family, for example, is less likely to move if a better job requires it.[27]

A further reinforcement of the circle comes on the street. After school the slum youngster "hangs around" somewhere. It might be in the nourishing atmosphere of a boys' club or a church group or a YMCA. But more likely it is on the street corner. It might or might not be with a delinquent gang. But almost certainly the group shares many life-shaping characteristics: aimlessness, lack of enthusiasm for school, doubts that they will achieve the success symbols portrayed in the magazine ads, resentment of the representatives of middle class life, need to feel important. Results of this combination will probably not be the kind of thing propagandists for the American way want to write about. Defeat and surrender to a low level of living are likely, as are obstreperous revolt and trouble with the law, parents, teachers, and everybody else.

In short, there are many real barriers to getting ahead and getting out of the slums. These reinforce each other at every turn and thus produce in the child or youth attitudes toward himself and the world that make him less and less capable of succeeding. He lives in an environment of failure, and tends either to give up, quit trying (if he ever started), and accept a level of life far far below the human potential, or to thrash about trying to achieve status in ways that are in fact self-defeating.

The marvel is that some people do succeed. Just how they do, and what the source of their strength are, is still a puzzle.

Racial concentration

Practically all of America's largest cities lost population between 1950 and 1960. Practically all of the largest cities became darker in color. Many whites moved out and up into the outlying fringe and suburban areas, leaving lower income whites, Negroes, Puerto Ricans, and Mexicans behind. These groups are contained in sharply defined zones. A certain area of the North Side in Chicago is where the newcomer southern mountain whites live. Everyone knows this. East Los Angeles is a Mexican area. In East Harlem, Puerto Ricans have replaced and are continuing to replace Italians. In San Antonio, the Mexicans live in the eastern part of town; in Phoenix, the South Side.

This is a familiar pattern and has come to be too easily

accepted as an ineluctable natural phenomenon. It probably is, to some degree. Hungarians live together at first, and sometimes for a long time. Germans stick together; witness Yorkville, New York City. The same is true for Jews, Italians, Poles. This is not all bad. After all, some cultural differentiation is a healthy thing in any society. In fact, one of the things to worry about in our developing mass society is the increasing erasure of cultural differences within a homogenizing social setting.

But where the cultural or ethnic difference is a prime indicator of a lower place on the social and economic scale and remains this way for a long time, there is trouble. Where the cultural and ethnic background is compounded by skin color, the trouble is worse and harder to overcome. This is the big difference between today's inhabiters of the slum ghettoes and those of thirty and forty years ago. The slum ports of entry into the big city where the Jews and Italians and Poles and Irish went when they landed are now the places where Negroes predominate. The former immigrants (the Negro newcomers to the city are called in-migrants) clustered together and were isolated for a while by their inability to speak English. But they or their children did learn to speak English, they got through more school in this country than they ever would have dreamed of in the old country, and by and large they succeeded. There are pockets of the old immigrants still left, but for the most part they have moved out. Their skin color did not bar them from access to better residential areas.

When the mayor of a large Middle Western city told a protest meeting of Negroes not long ago that they were then in the same situation he had been in some years before as an Irish immigrant and that it would be just a matter of time until they followed the same route he had, he was wrong. He was glossing over the big difference color makes.

Ralph Ellison, a Negro, told something about that difference in a novel.

> I am an invisible man. No, I am not a spook like those who haunted Edgar Allen Poe; nor am I one of your Hollywood-movie ectoplasms. I am a man of substance, of flesh and bone, fiber and liquids—and I might even be said to possess a mind. I am invisible, understand, simply because people refuse to see me. . . . When they approach me they see only my surrounding, themselves, or figments of their imagination—indeed, everything and anything except me. . . . That invisibility to which I refer occurs because of a peculiar disposition of the eyes of those with whom I come in contact. A matter of the construction of their *inner* eyes, those eyes with which they look through their physical eyes upon reality. . . . You're constantly being bumped against by those of poor vision. Or again you doubt if you really exist. . . . It's when you feel like this that, out of resentment, you begin to bump people back. And, let me confess, you feel that way most of the time. You ache with the need to convince yourself that you do exist in the real world, that you're a part of all the sound and anguish, and you strike out with your fists, you curse and you swear to make them recognize you. And, alas, it's seldom successful.[28]

In 1910, the proportion of the foreign born in America was 15 per cent, and another 20 per cent of the population had at least one foreign-born parent. Today about 7 per cent of the population is foreign born, and 16 per cent have one or more foreign-born parent. Ten per cent of the population is Negro.

Some interesting studies have been made about what people think about the various groups who have been in the stream of population movement. In 1935, Princeton students ranked groups as follows, from highest to lowest: Americans, English, Germans, Irish, Italians, Japanese, Jews, Chinese, Turks, Negroes.

Americans were characterized as "industrious, intelligent, materialistic, ambitious, and progressive." Negroes were thought of as "superstitious, lazy, happy-go-lucky, ignorant, and musical." [29] These stereotypes still exist today and influence the possibilities of Negroes moving to non-ghetto residential areas. What are the facts about color and residential patterns?

Between 1950 and 1960, nearly three-quarters of the largest metropolitan areas had increasing proportions of nonwhite residents. This was true of 90 per cent of such areas outside the South. In the South, only 35 per cent of the metropolitan areas experienced relative gains in numbers of nonwhites. Sixty per cent of them lost more Negroes than whites. [30]

Metropolitan areas include fringe and suburban areas as well as the cities themselves. What happened *within* the city borders? Without exception each of the fifty American cities of 250,000 population or more, regardless of their regional location, showed increases in the proportion of nonwhites in 1960 over 1950. In some cities, such as Minneapolis, St. Paul, and El Paso, the increase was modest. In many cities the changes were substantial. Newark, New Jersey, for example, changed from 17.2 per cent to 34.4 per cent nonwhite; Washington, D.C., from 35.4 per cent to 54.8 per cent. (Washington is the first large city to have a majority Negro population.)

In the twelve largest American cities the proportion of resident whites has fallen slightly but steadily since 1930 while the proportion of nonwhites has steadily increased, doubling in the thirty-year interval, 1930-1960. While the white population has become progressively more concentrated in the rings around the largest cities, the relative number of nonwhites in these rings (only 3 per cent in 1930) has grown by just two percentage points in thirty years.

The largest nonwhite percentage increase in the central cities occurred in the 1940s, while the losses in central city white population were most pronounced in the 1950s. There were many forces at work producing this result. Among them were fear, panic, discomfort, and uncertainty among whites as Negroes moved into the central city.

In 1910, eight out of ten Negroes lived in one or another of the eleven states of the old Confederacy. Over 90 per cent of these lived in rural areas. By 1940, the Negro population of the old Confederacy had increased only 12 per cent while the Negro population elsewhere in the United States had more than doubled, rising from 1.9 to 4 million. But the old Confederacy still contained more than two-thirds of all American Negroes.[31]

Between 1940 and 1960, the Negro population outside the South increased two and a quarter times—from 4 million to over 9 million, while the increase in the South was only 9 per cent. This increase outside the South, as noted above, was mainly in the central city areas. In 1960, the twelve largest central cities contained 31 per cent of all United States Negroes.

Within American cities there are clear and definite unwritten rules for the distribution of population by race. One universal rule is that racial concentrations are segregated.[32] In Chicago in 1950, 79 per cent of all Negroes lived in census tracts in which at least 75 per cent of all residents were Negro.

In 1960, it rose to 84.7 per cent. At the opposite end, 80 per cent of the non-Negroes in Chicago in 1950 lived in census tracts in which less than one per cent of the residents were Negro. Chicago's segregation pattern is somewhat extreme, but all cities follow the general pattern.

A second rule is that once a neighborhood begins to swing from white to Negro the trend is rarely reversed. Nor does a neighborhood with a substantial number of Negro residents, say 25 per cent, retain its mixed character over a long period of time.

A third rule is that the pattern of Negro residential expansion is from the core of the city outward. A fourth is that the Negroes move into neighborhoods already characterized by high residential mobility.[33]

In 1958, the Commission on Race and Housing reported:

> In the larger cities, especially of the north and west, the minorities have typically lived concentrated in the oldest sections of each city, districts abandoned by previous groups, with buildings deteriorated through age and neglect. Continual migration into these areas, together with the poverty of the residents and their exclusion from other districts, has generated a chronic shortage of housing available to minority groups. This, in turn, has intensified the slum conditions through crowding and over-use of the buildings.[34]

Robert Weaver, in *The Negro Ghetto*, said, "Two of the most outstanding (bad situations constantly getting worse) are the acceleration of the development of single class and racially restrictive neighborhoods and the possibility of their becoming enduring impediments to the solution of the problems of adequate shelter and racial harmony.'[35]

A classical study of Negroes in the city was carried out as a series of WPA research projects under the direction of W. Lloyd Warner and Horace Cayton of the University of Chicago and reported by Cayton and St. Clair Drake in the book *Black Metropolis*. Richard Wright's introduction to that book is a literary and social document that should be read by anyone interested in this subject.

Drake and Cayton, like other writers before and after, allude to the earlier immigrant groups.

> The various groups of immigrants who came to Midwest Metropolis (Chicago) tended to congregate in colonies. Then as individuals and families learned to speak English, as they acquired an economic stake in the new country and lost their foreign habits, they steadily moved away from these areas of first settlement into more desirable areas of second settlement. Later, they or their children merged with the general population. The communities of the foreign born grow smaller year by year; but as they shrink and disappear, Negro neighborhoods assume increasing importance in terms of size and influence. Black Metropolis emerges as a significant factor in the life of Midwest Metropolis.[36]

In 1945, when *Black Metropolis* was published, 90 per cent of Chicago's Negroes lived within the confines of the black belt. Data from the 1960 census clearly show that minority groups still live in segregated patterns and that an overwhelming preponderance of them live in areas that rank low by any method of rating—economic, housing, or level of education. In other words, they remain in slums and gray areas.

These are new world ghettoes and represent one of the important reasons why the slum problem is still one of major concern in the United States.

A ghetto is an area in a city where certain types of people who are looked down on by the larger community are forced to live. Most people who live in slums are "forced" to live there by their circumstances and characteristics: they are un-skilled, poor, not knowledgeable about how to get ahead in American society, perhaps non-white, ill-educated, and trapped by housing restrictions.

Ghettoes are bad from every point of view and do not belong in a healthy society. They sharpen the lines between classes and castes. This goes against what should be the domi-nant trend in the United States: a more and more open society, more upward and outward movement. Any blocks to all people getting ahead should be regarded as things to be eliminated.

An increasing homogeneity of the population in the slums is taking place now. This makes it easier to identify people who come from the slums and easier to fall into the habit of thinking about them as "belonging" there. This in turn makes it harder for them to get out. The homogeneity reinforces the way slum dwellers think of themselves as being outside the pale and reinforces the tendencies of people on the outside to be alienated from and hostile toward those on the inside.

We value the fact that ours is a pluralistic society (*e pluri-bus unum*—out of many, one) built on the interaction of many different groups and interests. If the differentiation among groups is based on such things as geographic location, political orientation, religious affiliation, or professional or occupa-tional identification, the interaction, not without conflict, to be sure, is workable and can result in a viable society. If, on the other hand, the differences between groups become too much characterized by qualities of have and have not, it is far more difficult to maintain the consensus essential to the existence of a nation. Anyone can think of dramatic instances where the overthrow of those in power has occurred in societies in which the gulf between haves and have nots was too wide.

It surprises many people hypnotized by our affluent society that an old chestnut like haves and have nots is still a matter for concern. Such surprise can come only from those who do not look around them. Many responsible people state the major problem of the entire world today in terms of the have and have not nations. They point to the fact that the rich nations are getting richer and the poor, poorer. This is not exactly analogous to the situation of the slums within an affluent society, but there are parallels.

Irving Shulman, in *West Side Story,* vividly tells about the process of ghetto formation and how the ghetto feels to those on the inside.

There was no place to move, no place to go. It was twenty years since the Second World War had begun and ended, but housing that ordinary people could afford was still at a premium; and if a white man wanted to get out of his apartment there wasn't a landlord anywhere who wasn't delighted at the vacancy which he could immediately fill at an increase in rent.

And if he wanted to subdivide three rooms into five, six, or even eight, he could fill every one of them with Puerto Ricans and really make himself a bundle so big and fat that he could spend most of any year in Florida or California. He need never see his buildings, his tenants, or do anything for the maintenance of halls, walls, and roofs. If the building fell down the landlord could turn his property into a parking lot.

None of the politicians lived on the West Side; none of them had to fight for a little room, a little air to breathe; and if the city was unsafe, crowded, depressing, if more and more streets were becoming unsafe after dark, whose fault was it? Not one person in any of the tenements had ever been asked if he wanted the PR's admitted to the country. They had no voice in the decision, but that didn't mean they didn't resent it.[37]

Low education and skill levels

The people who live in slums have not had much education and their occupational skills are limited. This is the great fact that must be changed if slums are to be changed.

It has already been demonstrated that income is low in the slums. The table on page 000 shows the typical clustering of low income, low education, low job status, and poor housing in several cities. These illustrations are characteristic of any large city in America.

In Detroit, education was related to income in 1957 as shown below.[38]

Education of Family Head	Median Family Income (dollars)
6 years or less	4,700
7 to 8 years	5,400
9 to 11 years	5,800
complete high school	6,500
college	8,100

The holder of a college degree had a 90 per cent chance of being employed for the full year, a high school graduate had 75 per cent, and a worker with fewer than nine years of schooling had only a 50 per cent chance.[39]

In the same city, the pupils in school were not performing

in a way that would presage a basic change in the situation in the future. Achievement levels in low income areas were substantially lower than those in higher income areas. School achievement, as measured by the standardized national tests, goes up with income.

In a school where the median family income ranged from $3,000 to $5,000, pupils in the sixth grade were achieving at grade levels ranging from 5.06 to 5.35. Where income was $5,000 to $7,000, the achievement levels ranged from 5.40 to 5.85. Where income was $7,000 to $9,000, achievement was 6.16 to 6.80. With income over $9,000, achievement was 6.95 to 7.50.[40]

In the San Francisco Bay area, a similar picture could be seen in 1959. Thirty-nine per cent of the males who earned less than $1,000 had fewer than eight years of schooling; 36 per cent of those earning between $1,000 and $2,000, 27 per cent of those earning $2,000 to $3,000, and 22 per cent of those earning $3,000 to $4,000 had the same schooling. In California, as a whole, thirty-three out of one hundred mothers receiving Aid to Dependent Children had only grade school education; forty-two had some high school; twenty were high school graduates; three had some college; one was a college graduate; one had no schooling at all. In New York, half the family heads receiving general relief had no more than six years of schooling.[41]

On the Lower East Side of New York City, where about 45 per cent of the school children are Puerto Rican and 15 per cent are Negro, 63 per cent of the 2,719 fourth and fifth grade pupils were reading six months or more below grade level. Among the Negro pupils alone, the figure was 63 per cent, among Puerto Ricans, 76 per cent, and among others 31 per cent. In the local high school, 57 per cent of the tenth and eleventh grade students were reading six months or more below grade level (Puerto Ricans, 84 per cent; Negroes, 67 per cent; others, 43 per cent). A substantial number of these young people were two, three, and four years behind.[42]

In 1962, the United States Department of Labor made some studies of unemployment among youth. These studies were based on related indices in low income census tracts in thirty-six cities across the country. These included all cities of over 500,000 population plus a few smaller ones, to give wider geographical representation. The broad outlines of the resulting picture were as expected: levels of income, education, and unemployment fluctuate together. In Brooklyn, for example, in the census tracts falling in the lowest quartile, the range of median income was $2,716-$5,324, and the range of educational achievement for the family head was 6.3 to 8.7 years of school. These are the slums of Brooklyn.[43] Unemployment in these same slum census tracts ranged from 6.3 per cent to 17.3 per cent, while the national rate was about 5.5 per cent. The unemployed are those of lowest skills.

In Manhattanville, a deteriorating area on New York City's West Side, the median number of school years completed ranged from 8.1 in one census tract to 12.1 in another.[44]

In the Hough section of Cleveland, a slum and deteriorating area, the level of occupations changed markedly between 1950 and 1960, along with the character of the population. In 1950, the total population of the area was 66,000 of whom 2,500 were Negro. In 1960, the total population was 72,000 of whom 53,000 were Negro. In 1960, 60 per cent of the wage earners were in blue collar occupations; in 1960, 82 per cent. In 1950, 62 per cent of the residents of the area over age twenty-five had not completed high school, while in 1960 the figure was 74 per cent. In 1950, the Hough area was not a high level area, but it was predominantly white. With the change to predominantly Negro, it went downhill and the concentration of indices of social pathology increased accordingly.[45]

In the low-income areas of the larger cities, school dropout rates get up as high as 70 to 80 per cent. The average for an entire big city is usually around 40 per cent but the average in the slum areas is much higher.

In Syracuse, New York, a study of the socioeconomic characteristics of the city was made by the Youth Development Center of Syracuse University in 1961. It measured occupation, education, home value, monthly rental, and condition of dwelling. Area Five came out worst on everything. It is an area of heavy Negro concentration, having the lowest median family income, $5,148. It is the principal slum of Syracuse. Here one-tenth of the population is "functionally illiterate" (has less than five years of schooling). Seventy-three per cent have not completed high school, as against a rate of 52.9 per cent for the city as a whole. Fifty-two per cent of the workers in this area are low skilled as against 32.5 per cent for the entire city.[46]

Atlanta, Georgia, looked at its slum population and found the same patterns.[47] A study grouped neighborhoods and ranged the groups according to levels of education, occupation, income, housing tenure, condition of housing, overcrowding, race, unemployment, women in the labor force, male unemployment, and age-group distribution. In 1959 in the lowest grouping, the slums, 46.7 per cent to 77.8 per cent of the adults over twenty-five in the census tracts had not gone beyond the eighth grade. In the best tract in this area 60 per cent of the families earned $5,000 per year or less and in the worst, 96.6 per cent earned less than $5,000. In this same area from two-thirds (67.8 per cent) to nearly all (97.1 per cent) of the men in each tract were employed in blue collar occupations. Over one-half of the housing units are deteriorating or dilapidated.

Slums rarely breed scientists, political leaders, professors, or brokers. They are efficient producers of low-skill, low-wage workers, of the last hired, first fired, of daily grist for the police mill, of cases for the welfare worker. Is this so because the people who live in the slums, the children who are born there, are intrinsically less capable? It is not.

Not everyone agrees that life in the slums has a deadening effect on the development of human powers. One of the best-known governors of the state of Georgia publicly stated that slum life has a strengthening effect on people. There is also the American myth of "slum kid to President" that clouds the thinking of many people.

Being born or raised in a slum area presents one with two strikes before the first pitch. Far fewer slum children succeed than others. The qualification here is that all slums are not the same, nor are all slum dwellers the same. There are among the poor those who are more upwardly mobile than others. There are those who have some combination of inner strengths and family encouragement, or who somehow have caught the vision of what life can hold beyond the crowded streets, who do achieve notably. But it is easy to be misled by such cases into erroneous conclusions about what happens to most of the people from the slums. Most of the people from the slums are to some degree crippled by their experience. This is another of the powerful reasons that the slum problem is now being raised to high priority for national concern.

The technological explosion in production, distribution, and servicing calls for more skilled manpower than heretofore needed. The skilled workers needed to keep the American economy expanding will not come from the slums in significant numbers. The pace of technological advance is such that we shall soon be faced with a surplus of labor. There will be a shortage of highly skilled people at the top of the pyramid and a surplus of people at skill levels further down. Some even speak of the necessity for the invention of "alternatives to work" when the goods we can consume can be produced, distributed, and serviced by machines to such a degree that men are hardly needed in the process. This is in the future, but it may not be too distant.

Putting this complex and grave question aside for the moment, let us assume an expanding domestic market, an expanding international market, and productive processes that need men. Even if government, business leaders, and scientists are able to make the policy and technical decisions that will keep the economy growing and demanding skilled workers, the slums are not going to be the source of these workers.

All this adds up to the desertion of the inner city by elements of strength and growth, leaving behind the weakest elements, who are joined by newcomer in-migrants who themselves have substantial obstacles to overcome before they can make their way in the big city, if they ever can.

Welfare cases

It comes as no surprise that families who receive public assistance of one kind of another are concentrated in poor areas. Statistics bear out the truism.

In East Woodlawn, a deteriorating Negro area in Chicago just south of the University of Chicago, 25 per cent of the 60,000 residents received financial help in 1962 under Aid to Dependent Children, Old Age Assistance, General Assistance, Disability Assistance, or Aid to the Blind.[48] Probably an additional 10 per cent received unemployment compensation.

In 1960, 51.6 per cent of Milwaukee's Aid to Dependent Children case load was concentrated in the inner city problem area, which has 10 per cent of the county population. The dependency rate in the area was double that for the whole county.

In Boston in 1962, the recipients of Aid to the Families of Dependent Children (formerly Aid to Dependent Children) were concentrated in the Roxbury, South End, and Charlestown areas. These are the three major slum areas of the city. In Roxbury, where the median family income ranges by census of 91,000 received A.F.D.C. assistance. In Charlestown, where the income range is $3,893—$5,984 the proportion is 4.3 tract from $2,750 to $6,003, 12.7 per cent of the population per cent. In the South End, with an income range of $3,163—$4,705, it is 6.1 per cent. Of the total population of Boston 3.9 per cent are on A.F.D.C.[49]

An analysis of the families receiving home relief in Manhattan, New York City, shows 72 per cent of the cases located in 30 per cent of the health areas of the borough—in other words, concentrated.[50] For the city as a whole, ninety-seven health areas with 27 per cent of the total population accounted for 73 per cent of the A.F.D.C. caseload. In Harlem, one out of four children under eighteen is supported by public assistance.[51]

The Hough area of Cleveland had less than 3 per cent of the A.F.D.C. cases in the city in 1956. In 1961, 28 per cent were there.

Internal mobility

A hypothetical aerial view of a slum would show it looking like an ant heap with much movement back and forth and in circles, but not much out of the area.

There are no studies showing the exact nature of this phenomenon authoritatively and exhaustively, but the testimony of close observers is persuasive. Principals of schools in low income areas, for example, throw up their hands at the fluctuations of their pupil registration. In Chicago's near North Side, where in-migrants from the southern Appalachians have concentrated, a school of 1,000 pupils had 1,500 transfers in and out in 1962.

The Hough area has a similar problem. The Youth Service Planning Commission of Cleveland had this to say about it.

> There is widespread knowledge that residents are on the move. With greater vacancy rates in apartments, families have been more free to select and improve their circumstances. Landlords complain about "rent skipping" and trailer rental outlets do a brisk business between sundown on Friday and sunrise on Monday.[52]

Data from four elementary schools in the area are shown in Table 4.[53]

Table 4—Enrollment Fluctuation in One School Year

School	Enrollment	Transfers In and Out	Per Cent Transferring
Dunham	1,999	1,865	93.3
Crispus Attucks	1,554	1,635	105.2
Wade Park	1,774	1,495	84.3
Hough	1,478	1,648	111.5

The East Woodlawn area of Chicago was marked by residential instability with moving rates higher among Negroes than among whites. Only 23.7 per cent of the Negroes five years and older had resided five years or longer in the same house, at the time of the 1960 census. The comparable figure for whites over the city as a whole was 50.9 per cent. This is characteristic of slum areas in all large cities. The Newark, New Jersey Mayor's Committee on Human Relations, in *Newark, a City in Transition,* stated that 62 per cent of the white households had moved at least once in the ten years between 1949 and 1959. The figures for Negroes was 84 per cent and for Puerto Ricans, 100 per cent. Forty-three per cent of the last moves by Negro families in the ten years were from the Central Ward, where 59 per cent of the population is in the lowest socio-economic grouping. Most of these moves were slightly up in the slum scale, but not out.

Crime

The fact that the most crime originates in slums has been known for a long time. In this country, scientific confirmation of what was "known" for centuries began in 1912, with Sophonisba P. Breckenridge and Edith Abbott, two social work pioneers. They made spot maps of the residences of juvenile delinquents and found them concentrated in low income, central city areas.[54]

This study was amplified and organized in relation to the general pattern of the city by Clifford Shaw and Henry D. McKay in their ground-breaking study.[55] They reached five major conclusions still regarded as valid in broad outline today.

1. Delinquency rates vary widely in different neighborhoods.

2. The rates are generally highest near the center of the city and decrease with distance from the center; they are also high near industrial and commercial subcenters.

3. Areas with high truancy rates also have high juvenile court case rates, adult commitments to county jail, and high delinquency among girls.

4. The areas with high rates in 1920 had high rates in 1900, although the ethnic composition of the area had changed almost completely. The rates remained the same for the *area* whether it was occupied by Poles, Germans, Italians, or Swedes.

5. The delinquency rate for particular national groups, such as German or Polish, showed the same general tendency as the rate for the entire population: to be high near the center of the city and low toward the outskirts. The rate for Negroes on the South Side of Chicago decreased regularly by square mile areas from 19.4 per cent near the center of the city to 3.5 per cent five miles from the center.

Edwin Sutherland utilized this information in developing his thesis that "crime is a response to the general culture which has been developing during the last two centuries." [56]

At present there are reasonable estimates that in slums comprising something like 20 per cent of the average American city's residential area occur 45 per cent of the major crimes, 55 per cent of the juvenile delinquency, and 50 per cent of the arrests.

Gus Tyler, in writing about organized crime, had some trenchant things to say about how this comes about.

> Poverty breeds revolt—and where a gang of youth is raised in poverty, it is doubly destined to organize against the outside world. To the struggle of young versus old is added the further dimension of poor versus rich. The world becomes two worlds; the world of "we" versus the world of "they." The "they" may mean many things: the rich and the virtuous, the cops and the courts, the folks on the other side of the tracks or other side of the street. The "they" represents money, power, and the dress and manners that go with these posts of status. The "they" is a thing to imitate in burlesque, for to imitate in reality is futile. The "they" is the enemy in an undeclared war. . . . The gang is composed in the bowels of the slum subculture. Unable to achieve status in the traditional manner, the gang creates its own standards—its new concept of true status . . . The delinquent culture becomes an inner frontier, raising barbarians in our midst, strange and hostile to our larger civilization. Out of this culture comes the young gang that in adulthood becomes part of organized crime, either by absorption or by conquest.[57]

This does not mean that all boys in delinquent gangs become adult criminals. They do not. Marriage and maturity take many delinquents into conventional lives. Likewise, not all delinquents have equal access[58] to apprenticeship in organized crime. But the theme so powerfully stated by Tyler remains true for the American city.

In the mid-nineteen-thirties a slum area of Cleveland was

thoroughly studied to ascertain its "social costs" for the city. In this area where 2.5 per cent of the total city population was located, were 21.3 per cent of the murders and 26.3 per cent of the houses of prostitution. The cost of police protection per family was $57.60 as against $18.12 for the city as a whole. In the Hough area of Cleveland in 1960, there were 22 major crimes per 1,000 population. In the city as a whole there were only 9.8.[59]

In Milwaukee, a 1960 study of the "inner core area" showed that both juvenile delinquency and adult crime were disproportionately high. In the inner core, which had 13.7 per cent of the city population in 1957, the proportions of adult arrests in the area were as follows: murder, 60 per cent, rape, 48 per cent; robbery, 21 per cent; aggravated assault, 69 per cent; burglary, 38 per cent; other assault, 47 per cent; forgery, 41 per cent; embezzlement, 20 per cent (embezzlement is a white collar crime); commercial vice, 72 per cent; narcotics, 67 per cent; drunkenness, 22 per cent; intoxicated driving, 16 per cent.[60]

A 1957 study of 9,238 white boys in Nashville, Tennessee, deepened the analysis of where and why delinquency and crime take place.[61] This study showed that the relationship of social status, class, or rank and delinquency is not simple. The status structure of the residential area and the traditions of the area have much to do with whether or nor or how deeply a boy becomes committed to a criminal way of life. The largest proportions of delinquents are found in those areas of more homogeneous social status, low in rank. The boys who are oriented toward delinquency and crime are from the lower status groups. These boys tend to be conforming non-achievers. Delinquency as a form of group behavior (peer-oriented) is the most common form of delinquent organization among both lower and middle status levels.

In New York City in 1960, ninety-seven health areas of the city containing 27 per cent of the total population accounted for 51 per cent of the juvenile delinquency. These same areas were high on all other measure of "problems" as well: infant mortality, dependency, venereal disease, and the like.[62]

This "badness" in the slums tends to drive out the "good" and speed the spread of the slums. It is another reason to regard the slum problem as a serious one. Slums have a way of spreading. Until our society is able to arrange that the gulf between those who are "up" and those who are "down" is less wide and less difficult to cross, they are likely to continue. The spread takes place within the city proper in areas contiguous to existing slums, and increasingly it will happen in outlying areas. More and more we are likely to see enlarging splotches of deteriorating housing zones as a part of the suburban picture.

Within the city proper slums and gray areas discourage the establishment and growth of the facilities and institutions which themselves help to stem the tide of further deterioration. This applies equally to industrial, commercial, and cultural institutions. The slum specter is not the only influence in this cycle, but it is an important one. Additional influences in the movement of industries out of the inner city are the fact that they no longer need to be near the rail heads and sidings of the city, the mechanical efficiencies to be derived from single-floor operations, the availability of utilities in outer areas, the relative ease of assembly of land for plants and the availability of clerical workers outside the inner city.

Commercial and service operations of many kinds, particularly retail sales, are pulled out of the city by the suburban movement of the population with highest purchasing power.

The fact of the slums drives productive and strengthening institutions out of the city, too. Slum dwellers are people of lowest skill. They do not represent a prized source of labor. This is becoming ever more true. In the old days a pool of unskilled, cheap labor was an important consideration in the location of industry. With the rapid pace of technological advancement, the demand is now moving to people of higher skill, and the unskilled are becoming surplus.

Slum dwellers are poor people and don't represent effective demand for consumer goods. Therefore the distributors of consumer goods follow the demand, and move out. Slum dwellers are people of limited intellectual and cultural horizons. Therefore the institutions catering to the interests of people who read, go to plays, and value art and music are not found in the slums. One of the magnets of the big city is the fact that it can support intellectual and cultural institutions because of its large and varied population. But the patrons of such institutions generally don't live in the poor parts of town. They live in the upper class, expensive, city areas or in the suburbs, and travel back to the city to soak up their organized culture. They do not like to go through the slums to get there, however. It is too unpleasant and dangerous. If the slums begin to encroach, the cultural institutions are likely either to lend their weight to urban renewal plans to wipe out a particular slum (moving the people to some other slum or creating a new one for them) and to replace it with a "civic center," or to relocate the institution itself in a nicer place.

A similar thing happens with churches and other kinds of people-serving agencies. There has been a steady outward movement of churches. This is natural enough, since the church-supporting people are headed for the suburbs. A number of church groups have a bad conscience about this. They feel that perhaps there is an element of running away from the very needs and problems churches ought to be concerned with. However, there are now active efforts to maintain church activity in the city proper. These take the form of "inner city missions," or special efforts to train ministers for slum work, or invention of more effective ways of serving slum people. The active role of church leaders in the 1963 civil rights demonstrations was a reflection of this.

Many leisure-time organizations and case work agencies are faced with a similar dilemma. They often find that the residents of the lower income parts of the city do not readily take advantage of their facilities or services. The organizations that offer building or club programs are often puzzled by the fact that the people who need them most just do not use them. They find themselves serving a middle class clientele, or at least those who are already striving hard to become middle class.

A basic tenet of the case work agencies is that they cannot serve clients who do not want to be served, who are not ready to be helped to help themselves. Most slum dwellers feel their most pressing needs are very immediate and material. They may, in fact, be much in need of personal counseling, but they usually do not seek this until they know where enough money is going to come from, who is going to take care of the children while the mother works, who will pay the medical bills when the father's workmen's compensation runs out. Therefore, if agencies of this kind make scatter maps of where their clients live, they are likely to find them in the wealthier parts of the city. They do not effectively serve the population of the slum.

The existence and spread of slums and gray areas accelerate the flow of middle class people out of the city and discourage such people from coming back. Not everyone in America wants to live in a split-level house, surrounded by a lawn, in a suburb. Some people, other things being equal, would really like to stay in the city. They like apartments where they do not have to worry about maintenance, or arrange for oil deliveries, or put up screens. They like to be near downtown shops, and art galleries, restaurants, museums, antique shops, second-hand book stores, and the like. But when they see the slum advancing relentlessly toward their house or older apartment building, they get nervous, particularly when they have children. Most middle class people expect their children to go to college. To get into college (and stay there) students require a solid foundation of elementary and high-school education. The slum school does not provide it. This is a powerful push toward the better schools of the suburbs. Suburban schools are not always better, but they usually are, and everybody thinks they are.

Even the childless couple or parents returning to the city after the children have grown up are going to be nervous about the encroaching slum or gray area. They have visions of being mugged at night; they fear to enjoy the nearby park; they expect to find the tires on their car slashed. With worries like these, which may be fully justified, they are not disposed to wait and see what happens. The "bad" drives them out, too.

Health problems

In a city where slums represent about 20 per cent of the residential area as much as 50 per cent of the disease will be in that area. The Hough section of Cleveland is such an area. There the death rate from influenza and pneumonia is 44.7 per 100,000 population as against a rate of 29.7 for the city as a whole. Stillbirths are at the rate of 28.7 per 1,000 live births, compared with a city rate of 17.9. The accidental death rate is among the highest in the city. These are health problems related to poverty.

In the inner core area of Milwaukee, in 1958, the infant mortality rate was 29 per cent higher than for the city as a whole. The tuberculosis death rate was 54 per cent higher than for the whole city. In New York City, areas containing 27 per cent of the total population accounted for 45 per cent of the infant deaths, and 71 per cent of the venereal disease.

A seven-year study of mental health and environmental factors in midtown New York (population 170,000, 99 per cent white, wide range of social and economic status) showed a strong connection between social and economic status and mental health. Persons of low status have more mental illness than persons of middle or high status. This runs counter to the popular notion of the high status executive with ulcers or the organization man as the people with the mental health problems. This may be true with reference to neurosis, but not with reference to more serious mental illness. In this study, 13 per cent of the people of low status were classified as probable psychotic types while only 3.6 per cent of the high status people were so classified.[63]

In late 1963, tuberculosis, generally assumed to be conquered, began a comeback. The New York City Health Department announced a 12 per cent increase in the disease over the previous year. As reported in the New York *Times* of September 27, "The sharpest increases are in disadvantaged areas—among Negroes and Puerto Ricans—particularly children under the age of ten. There were also increases in the white community, but these were mostly minimal cases." People in the slums are sicker.

Broken families

One of the things that may help a child of the slums to overcome the tremendous handicaps that are his from birth is a strong family base—a family in which there is love and respect, ambition and aspirations on the part of the parents for the children, support and encouragement for them in their school work, or getting a job, or withstanding the neighborhood temptations.

Very many families in the slums are not able to provide this kind of matrix for their youngsters. In many cases there simply is not what could be called a real family in the first place. The parents may never have been married, or they may be divorced. The system of serial monogamy (one man after another but one at a time) is not uncommon. Among Negroes a matriarchal pattern is the usual one. During slavery women had to be the heads of their families—the men were often sold to other places. Today, Negro men still have difficulty being heads of families because they cannot find or qualify for good, steady jobs. Women can often find employment more easily than men and make more money.

Life in the slums tends to be one crisis after another—
unemployment, followed by illness, followed by arrest, followed by some other crisis until the cycle starts all over
again. This does not make for stability and growth and
development. These are characteristics of families of lowest
status. Among people of somewhat higher status, "working
class" family cohesiveness is more likely to be present although
still not in the same degree nor in the same way as in the
usual, middle class family. For example, in a working class
culture, families are not so likely to seek recreation and enter-
tainment or socializing as a family unit as are middle class
families.

> During a lower class child's life with his parents, they are
> likely to separate several times, with extramarital partnerships
> common for both parents. His mother may live with several
> men, and other members of the family may also frequently
> have extramarital affairs. Since the mother is usually at work,
> she cannot prevent the sexual play of her children in their
> unsupervised excursions. Illegitimate births account for one-
> fourth to one-third of all lower class births, and delinquency is
> far higher than in the lower-middle class. School retardation is
> almost universal; after all, the parents have attended only a
> few grades in school.[64]

In a study of social influences on IQ, Martin Deutsch and
Bert Brown found many more broken homes among lower
status people than among higher. They selected a cross-section
sample in New York City including all social levels. "One
of the most striking differences between the Negro and white
groups is the consistently higher frequency of broken homes
and resulting family disorganization in the Negro group. In-

deed this phenomenon varies directly with social class *and* with race." [65]

Among the three social level groupings the percentages of families in which the father was not in the home were as shown in the accompanying chart.

	White	Negro
Lowest	15.4	43.9
Middle	10.3	27.9
Highest	0.0	13.7

A study of the New York City West Side Urban Renewal area [66] (39 per cent median family income below $5,000 as against city-wide rate of 36 per cent) showed 20.3 per cent of the adult population either separated or divorced as against a city-wide rate of 9.6 per cent. One out of three Harlem children under eighteen lives in a broken home.

In East Woodlawn, Chicago, a predominantly Negro area, 16.1 per cent of the males and 22 per cent of the females are separated or divorced. The city-wide rate is 11 per cent for nonwhite males and 4.2 per cent for white males; 19 per cent for nonwhite females and 4.9 per cent for white females. Forty-two per cent of the families in East Woodlawn have incomes of less than $4,000.

In the Homewood-Brushton area of Pittsburgh, 21.8 per cent of the families did not have husband and wife both present, compared with 18.8 per cent for the city as a whole. Twenty-six and four tenths per cent of Homewood-Brushton children do not live with both parents, as compared with 16.6 per cent for Pittsburgh at large. Broken homes are everywhere, but there are more in the slums.

Relocation

With the onset of urban renewal in the central cities and with new highway construction, relocation has become a fact of life for many slum dwellers and a monster to be contended with. When cities are "renewed" and limited access highways built, it is not well-off people who have to be moved, it is the poor. The homes of the poor are in the way and must be demolished to make room for highways, office buildings, and middle income housing. Since 1949, nearly 700 cities have received approval for almost 1,400 urban renewal projects.

About 80 per cent of the people who have been relocated are Negro. This has presented a political, economic, and human problem, which has resulted in a change of emphasis in the federally-supported urban renewal programs from "bull-dozing" to conservation, rehabilitation, and spot clearance. In the past, the clearance operation simply moved the slum from one place to another, even though the majority of relocatees moved to better (and more expensive) housing. The relocation process is expensive for the people involved even though there are moving allowances. It is inconvenient, it shatters neighborhood relationships, and it ruins neighborhood small businesses. The resentment occasioned by relocation has made it one of the most difficult aspects of renewal for local elected officials who don't like to have people mad at them. Professional groups have become disaffected because of the hardships imposed on the relocatees, and the breaking up of neighborhood "cultures" that provide social relationships and mutual support in many slum areas.

In practically no urban renewal experience to date have

the former residents of an area been moved back there after the new construction has been completed. Most of the new residential construction has been financially out of reach of the former residents. People like to move, but they don't want to be pushed.

Inadequate services

Even though slums cost cities more in direct service expenditures for police protection, fire fighting, garbage removal, welfare, and health, these services always prove inadequate.

The New York State Division of Housing in 1958 estimated that slums, representing 20 per cent of the average American city's residential area, cost taxpayers 45 per cent of all city service expenditures and still produce excessive health, welfare, housing, crime, and fire problems.[67]

We have seen that slum residents are poorly educated and the pattern is being perpetuated in their children, yet expenditures for schooling in these areas are less than elsewhere. Patricia Sexton, in *Education and Income,* summarized the situation.

A great deal more money is now being spent by the schools of Big City in upper income areas. Certainly an argument can be made that in a democratic society the reverse of this should be true, since need is greater in lower income areas. Present inequalities in school expenditures are: Dropouts: In one low income high school alone, $192,000 was saved in one year on drop-outs. Education for lower income students is therefore costing much less than the education of upper income students, who rarely drop out of school before graduation.

Buildings and facilities: It is obvious from our data that a great deal more money has been spent for school buildings and facilities in upper income areas.

Teachers: Considerably more money is being spent on teachers' salaries in upper income schools since substitutes and inexperienced teachers, who are heavily concentrated in low income areas, are paid less in wages and fringe benefits than regular experienced teachers.

Club activities: Indications are that most of the advantages of club activities go to upper income students. These activities take up a great deal of teacher time and are therefore costly.

Gifted child programs: These costly programs service upper income students almost exclusively.

Evening school, summer school, parent groups, adult activities: Since these services are provided disproportionately to upper income groups, whatever costs are involved, in either teacher time or more direct expenditures, are being unequally distributed.

Another related cost item: Each year about $3.6 billion is spent on higher education at the college and university level; this amounts to about one dollar for every four and a half spent on public school education. Most of this money comes from public subsidies, though seldom from local board of education funds. Most of this $3.6 billion is being spent on upper income students, who make up the bulk of the college population.[68]

Alfred J. Kahn had this to say with reference to community services for children in trouble, which usually means slum children.

From state to state and locality to locality the situation repeats itself: There are too few probation officers, detention facilities are overcrowded, courts lack clinical diagnostic resources, there are too few qualified remedial reading teachers, guidance clinics cannot recruit enough trained social workers, training schools are too large and crowded beyond recommended capacities, there are no casework treatment resources for highly disorganized families, and so on.[69]

Kahn does not conclude that we need more of everything. He goes on to say: "While constantly strengthening existing programs we must continue to ask where we need *more* facilities and where different *kinds* of programs." Services alone will not make the difference but the slums do not even have enough services of the kind we do know how to provide.

In spite of the inadequacy of services, slums cost taxpayers more money. Nobody has ever seriously denied that slums represent an economic drain on the city. Usually, where one or another kind of action has been taken locally concerning slums, this has probably been as persuasive a motivating argument as any. It is very difficult to prove the case down to the last decimal point and beyond the reach of methodological critics, but the basic truth is well established.

A number of studies made in the nineteen-thirties did a fair job of building the case.[70] Their objective was to show that slum areas took more revenue out of the city government than they put into it. Most of them were made to support public housing programs. There have been no recent studies of this kind.

In Indianapolis, in a slum area of 1,500 population, health, crime, and fire costs totaled $92,775 as against property tax revenues of $11,312.30—a net outflow of $81,462.70.

In Cleveland, six slum census tracts were analyzed. For this population of 22,000 the cost of direct services was $1,356,988, while the tax income, all of which was not paid, was $225,035 —a net cost of $1,131,953.[71]

A study by the Boston City Planning Board in 1934 concluded that the business district and high rental residential district gave the city a large surplus; the industrial and medium rent districts a small one; the suburban district, with detached houses, showed a small deficit; and the low rent area showed a large one.

A 1936 study in St. Louis showed that the slums are subsidized directly by the higher value residential districts, and the central downtown business dictrict.[72]

Another study in Newark, New Jersey,[73] set out to examine those items where it seemed likely that per capita expenditure would be greater for the slums than for the good neighborhoods. Each of these items (health, welfare, education, fire fighting, and police protection) was examined to determine the amounts spent in the areas studied. Each dwelling in the slum area cost the city $338.10 per year more than the revenue per dwelling while the very good residential district yielded, per dwelling, $420.13 more in taxes each year than the cost of providing its services.

In Columbus, Ohio,[74] the conclusions were of the same order. The purpose of that study was to determine whether or not a deteriorated area was an economic loss to the city as a whole. The result: the net cost to the city for the slum area was $24,420 while the high income suburb contributed an excess income to the city treasury of $176,099 over and above the cost of services received.

All of these studies are deficient to some degree, in that completely unassailable methods of analysis and allocation of costs have not yet been developed. But methods are sound enough so that it can be said confidently that slums are an economic drain on municipal resources.

Skid row

Almost all of the large cities of America have a skid row section where lone men live in dormitories or hotels, in tiny rooms or cubicles. These men are extremely poor. Their death rate is 6.5 times that of the general death rate among white males.

The popular image of skid row is that it is the absolute bottom. There is no place to go from there but to the grave. The men on skid row as a group seem so derelict that there can be no hope of doing anything at all about the situation.

Recent, more thorough analyses of the men on skid row, and how they get there, are not quite so discouraging. These studies were inspired by the fact that urban renewal programs frequently run into skid row. If skid row is simply bulldozed, it moves somewhere else as long as the basic problems of the men (and some women) are not tackled.

There are four major causes for arrival on skid row.

1. Economic hardship. More men gravitate to skid row because of irregular employment than because of alcoholism.

2. Poor mental health. Deep personal maladjustment expressed in alcoholism, wanderlust, marital discord, and emotional instability affect 20-40 per cent of skid row men.

3. Poor social adjustment. Many of the skid row men are "marginal men" torn by conflicting cultures or religious beliefs, victims of social pressures and circumstances that made it difficult for them to make a normal social adjustment.

4. Poor physical health or disability. The disabled constitute a small but substantial group.[75]

Most of these "causes" operate in combination and frequently are mutually reinforcing.

About half of the men on skid row drink not at all or not excessively. Many of them are old-age pensioners who cannot afford to live in more expensive rooms. In the Chicago skid row, the men are classified as follows: [76]

A. Homeless men on skid row because of poverty
or other personal reasons

Classification		Per Cent
Elderly, no drinking problem		11.9
Nonalcoholic, employed		14.9
Nonalcoholic, unemployed		16.3
Disabled	9.7	
Not disabled	6.6	

B. Homeless men on skid row who are alcoholic
derelicts or heavy drinkers

Classification	Per Cent
Potential alcoholics	23.8
Problem alcoholics (heavy drinkers)	19.7
Alcoholic derelicts	13.0
Other	0.4

The presence of these men on skid row says not that *they* are hopeless, but that society has either given up on them and turned its eyes and resources in another direction, or has decided to quarantine this particular unpleasantness.

Skid row is now a place where a single man at the end of his rope can get a cheap room, a cheap drink, companionship of others who will not look down on him, and the limited uplift or maintenance services of Public Welfare, the Salvation

Army, and a variety of missions. There are very few instances of serious agency or institutional efforts to rehabilitate or even to provide adequate care for these men.

In Chicago, not less than $5.5 million per year is spent to assist or support homeless men. Most of this money goes to meet day-to-day sustenance costs, court costs, police costs, and administrative expenses. Less than 2 per cent goes toward trying to salvage the men, to reduce the size of the area, or to diminish the magnitude of the problem.

Some years ago, a half-reasonable case might have been made that skid row represented some kind of an economic asset to the city. It provided a pool of readily available, short term, unskilled labor. This has completely changed. Labor shortages are now at the middle and upper levels of skill and what demand there is for unskilled labor can readily be filled from the ranks of younger workers not yet weakened by age or the accumulated miseries that lead to skid row.

Skid row is now an economic liability both in terms of its human content and in terms of the valuable real estate it occupies. This real estate is usually located near the city center and could well be used for commercial, industrial, or residential redevelopment. The skid row area itself is thus an obstacle to healthier urban development and it poisons an extensive surrounding area because of its nature and because even drunkards can walk.

Isolation and alienation

Numerous studies of the attitudes and outlooks of slum residents have discovered widespread feelings of being "out," of having no control of their own lives or their surroundings, of isolation and alienation, of "anomie." The term anomie came into the language of sociology from Emile Durkheim, a French social scientist who used the concept in his classic study of suicide. Durkheim used the term to refer to the breakdown of norms or standards that govern the aspirations and behavior of individuals. Robert MacIver defined it as the "breakdown of an individual's sense of attachment to society." [77] Harold Lasswell calls it "the lack of identification on the part of the primary ego of the individual with a 'self' that includes others. In a word, modern man appeared to be suffering from psychic isolation. He felt alone, cut off, unwanted, unloved, unvalued." [78]

Leo Srole developed a scale for the measurement of anomie that includes five elements.

1. The individual's feeling that community leaders are detached from and indifferent to his needs.

2. The feeling that the social order is essentially fickle and unpredictable.

3. The individual's belief that he and people like him are going downhill: "In spite of what some people say, the lot of the average man is getting worse, not better."

4. The belief that life is meaningless: "It's hardly fair to bring children into the world with the way things look for the future."

5. The individual's feelings that his immediate circle of relationships is not comfortable and supportive: "These days a person doesn't really know whom he can count on." [79]

This scale gives a fair picture of the feelings of great numbers of people who reside in American slums. Srole called the sum of these feelings "one of the most pervasive and potentially dangerous aspects of Western society, namely the deterioration in the social and moral ties that bind, sustain and free us."

Harvey Zorbaugh, a sociologist and a persuasive writer, gave a strong impression of this feeling of alienation in his book *The Gold Coast and the Slums:*

> The common denominator of the slum is its submerged aspect and its detachment from the city as a whole. The slum is a bleak area of segregation of the sediment of society; an area of extreme poverty, tenements, ramshackle buildings, of evictions and evaded rents; an area of working mothers and children, of high rates of birth, infant mortality, illegitimacy, and death; an area of pawnshops and second hand stores, of gangs, of "flops" where every bed is a vote.
>
> The life of the slum is lived almost entirely without the conventional world. Practically its only contacts with the conventional world are through the social agency and the law. The social agency is looked upon as a sort of legitimate graft whereby small incomes may be considerably supplemented; and the law, symbolized by the "copper," the "bull," the "flivver," and the "wagon" is to the dweller in the slum a source of interference and oppression, a cause of interrupted incomes, a natural enemy. [80]

One big-city institution that has had some effect in reducing the isolation of parts of the low income population is the political machine. It provided an avenue for upward mobility for some people, particularly in the immigrant groups, who were not able or who chose not to move up through occupational or educational routes. Not infrequently the political machine was a force for integration in low income neighborhoods, providing a meeting place for people who had "competitive or indifferent relations with one another in other institutional settings." [81]

It also provided "welfare services" as part of the vote-getting process. In recent years, with the change in the nature of the slum population and the growth of professionalized relief and welfare services, it has had to find a new role. This has involved focusing on persons somewhat higher in the status system. These are usually people who are thought to represent or to be able to influence some group.

Democracy calls for all people having a voice in the process of government. If some people do not have an effective voice in government, or if they are not equipped through experience and education to express themselves in responsible and rational ways, or if they are disinterested, democracy is weakened.

Democracy is based on principles of justice and equality. When slum dwellers can see that the system they are in does not produce justice and equality for all, and that they are the ones who do not have justice and equality, they are likely to question the validity of the system and not to believe what the books say about it. Or at least they are less inclined to get out and vote for the best man and the best policies with the idealism teachers of civics would like to promote.

One of the pervasive characteristics of people in the slums, young and old, is that they have, and know full well that they have, less stake in things as they are, in the system, than their more fortunate fellow citizens. This doesn't mean that the slums are hotbeds of revolution. They are not. History tells us that most revolutions are made by middle class intellectuals. But blatant and widespread conditions of inequality and restricted opportunities are without doubt potential fuel for extremist solutions or for demagoguery such as that represented by the Black Muslim movement.

Dr. James B. Conant referred to the situation of youth in the slums as "social dynamite." He could as well have said political dynamite. Slums are a threat to democracy because it is hard for slum children to grow into adulthood as well-informed, interested, thoughtful, independent citizens. If the supply of informed and interested citizens is diminished, many of the critical decisions that must be made by voters and leaders will be wrong. They will be unduly influenced by ignorance, passions of the moment, and narrow or local interests, and increasingly will be made by the smaller numbers of people who have technical competence or who are in positions of power. Accountability for policies and decisions in today's fantastically complex world is more and more difficult to manage within a framework of democratic control. The problem is aggravated if a substantial part of the demos is ill equipped, or is isolated from or hostile to the established channels of political expression. This is a problem for our entire society. It is intensified for the slum population.

And so . . .

All of this seems to add up to a confused picture. There are broad generalizations that can be made about all slums. Within these generalizations occur many variations and differences from place to place and within the types of people who inhabit the slum.

There is danger, however, in focusing too much on the differences and the subtypes. The importance of knowing about idiosyncrasies is undeniable, but there is always the risk of making the analysis so refined, so sophisticated, so complex, and so idiosyncratic that remedial action seems impossible.

This implies that remedial action is desirable and possible. Very explicitly, that is the position taken in this book: the slums represent conditions inimical to a democratic society, and something can be done about it. It is important to be realistic about this and not to expect too much change too soon, or a reaction of despair and disillusionment will set in, as it has before in response to unsuccessful utopian or naïve efforts to "do something" about the slums.

Realism dictates that the big generalizations about slums be kept in the forefront when remedial action is being considered. Realism dictates that the thrust of remedial action be to open wider the doors leading out of the slum and to help people through them. Some will never make it, some do not want to make it, some cannot make it. For these, society will have to find its ways of accommodation, as it has since the city began. But if accommodation becomes society's sole response to the great bulk of the people now in the slums, the results can only be festering decay or explosion, or both.

Part II

RESPONSE

*WHAT TO DO ABOUT
IT: POSSIBILITIES
FOR POLICY
AND ACTION*

PROLOGUE

It is clear by now that this book chooses the *people* who live in the slums and the systems of life they are in as the prime targets of policy and action if slum conditions are to be changed. It does not recommend exhortation of slum people to straighten up and fly right, clean up and work hard, don't steal and fight and don't get sick. It does mean that the bad conditions in the slums will become better to the degree that the people who now inhabit the slums become less ignorant, have more money, have a chance to move up and out, have the opportunities to do so, and become aware that they have that chance.

Free choice an objective

Ours is a society based in large part on choice. However, to talk about everyone having "free individual choice" is vastly oversimplified and naïve, since the choices that many people are allowed to make or are capable of making are very limited. They are limited by the objective opportunities available. A thousand men could not choose to be skilled steel workers if there are only a hundred such jobs. They cannot choose such work if they do not have the skills or the basic education that will enable them to acquire the skills.

A thousand Negroes with incomes of more than $15,000 per year cannot move out of Harlem to Evanston, Scarsdale, Shaker Heights, or Grosse Point because these towns will resist them. They are also restrained by the fact that all Negroes do not want to be the first on the firing line. It takes great courage to break the color barriers. Not all Negroes want to live in predominantly white neighborhoods. There are many restrictions on free choice here.

Another restriction is the unwritten rules of your group. If your father is a university professor you are not supposed to aspire to be an air hammer operator on a street repair crew. It just isn't done and your peers will ostracize you, a painful experience. This restriction on free choice works the other way, too. If you are at the bottom of the social and economic ladder, our mythology notwithstanding, you are not expected to aspire too high. You will be thought silly, and in most cases, under present circumstances, you probably will be silly.

Nevertheless, free choice is an important determinant of what happens in the city. Transportation planners are as acutely aware of this as anyone. They can make elaborate arrangements for fast mass transportation in and around a big city, but they find that huge numbers of people will still choose to drive into the city in individual cars that choke the downtown streets.

One broad generalization can be made: *The objective of policy and action should be to make people better qualified to make free choices, and to increase the choices open to them.* This means choices about what job to have, where to live, how long to stay in school, what to do with spare time, whom to marry and when, how many children to have, and all the other choices, big and little, that cumulatively determine who and what a person is.

A man does not have free choice if he cannot read well enough to fill out an application form or follow simple written instructions about how to perform an industrial process. He does not have free choice if he is not hired because of his color or accent. He does not have free choice if he is spiritually imprisoned by an atmosphere of hopelessness or apathy among those around him. He does not have free choice if he is an unskilled person in an economy growing too slowly and distributing its rewards in a grossly inequitable manner. He does not have free choice if he is poor. Anti-slum policy and program must be judged by the degree to which it enables people really to have free choice.

Action in concert
an objective

Whatever is done had better be done in concert. The slum, like the city itself, is not a thing apart. It is the creature of history and of policies, of actions and conditions. It is affected directly by what happens somewhere else, or by what does not happen somewhere else.

Thoughts on what to do about the slums encompass more than just "action programs." They must encompass policies as well. Perhaps the policies are as important as the actions. Separation of the two has been one of the troubles with our efforts until now. Action programs become the property of people-who-do-good while policies are set by hard-headed-businessmen, political give and take, the conditions of the market, and the like.

While it is an utter waste of time to bank on a panacea, like public housing, for instance, to clean up and cure the slums, at the same time some things are more important than others. There are certain policies, actions, and approaches that have higher priority than others. There is risk in saying that slum problems are the result of many things and that therefore no one approach is going to solve them. The danger here is the tendency to move from that to saying that everything must be done if the problem is to be solved.

This is almost as fruitless as plumping for the single panacea. It leads to advocacy of "saturation": "If we, just for once, do everything we know how to do in this slum area, we will be able to improve it radically. We've never been given a chance. We've never had enough money to provide the services we know very well how to provide. If we just had enough money to give social and health services a fair chance, everyone would see how effective they can be."

The saturation approach fails to discriminate between more important things and less important things. The concept is too often limited to: "Let's put more of everything in." It is also defective in that it expects too much from services provided for the poor and maladjusted.

Thus the trick and the art involved here are to see the problems of the slum in all their breadth and interrelations, and to tackle them on this basis, but at the same time select the most effective individual weapons that will go into the battery. This selection is the hard part.

Clarity of goals

Certainly, when one is trying to think out a systematic approach to slum problems, he must choose realistic goals. These goals do not have to be spelled out in specific terms. This is difficult to do and it is not essential to progress. If one tries to do it, he can be both very wrong and utterly friendless. He can alienate comrades by trying to be too precise in his definition of where to go. Many attempts to plan utopias have been wrecked on the rocks of unforeseen developments, simple error, and human dynamism. Utopias still are seductive and even as recently as the last year of the Eisenhower administration an attempt was made to spell out "national goals." It did not succeed. The goals were sufficiently general that they offended no one and thus had little meaning.

With reference to housing, it is not necessary to establish a norm of desirable density. Some people even question the desirability of establishing allowable maximum densities, because they point out that the density itself does not necessarily make for bad housing. Density, of course, refers to the number of people per square foot of land, not people per room. In any case, spelling out how many people should be allowed per square measure of land may stimulate an argument that really is not worth the time. On the other hand, it is desirable to move against overcrowding.

It is not necessary or desirable, or possible, for that matter, to plan for an optimum level of family income. It is possible and necessary to establish levels of income, adjusted to local costs, below which no individual or family should be allowed to fall, but this is quite different from trying to identify optimum levels of income and arrange, wage, salary, and tax structures to achieve that particular level. Neither is the goal merely equality. It may be equality of opportunity, but not equality of status.

Given the complex nature of society, differing levels of human capacity, different talents among human beings, the fact that production and distribution processes require a division of labor, there are going to be different statuses. Some people will rank higher than others. Some will have more privileges, more honor, and more of the material things of life. And those near the top will be fewer in number than those lower down. No matter what kind of socio-economic system exists—communist, socialist, capitalist, mixed one way or another—any system that includes numbers of people is going to have some positions of high status and more of lower status.

Equality of status is not our goal. The goal is equality of opportunity to rise to higher status on the basis of effort and merit (and a "little bit of luck"). The goal is to avoid the assignment of high status by birth, by color, or by cheating.

Effective organization

Before getting into the specifics about some of the possible policies and actions, something should be said about organization and changeability. In this complicated world there is not any set pattern of organization that will guarantee efficiency and effectiveness. But there are some things to keep in mind about organization that will help to get things moving and to keep them moving in the right direction.

One thing is sure: The organization that is supposed to do

one thing or another about slum conditions should be near the place where the real decisions, those that govern the political and economic systems of the area involved, are made. Often, particular tasks of looking after some part of the city's machinery are assigned to commissions or other groups set somewhat apart from the daily business of running the city. This has been done basically for three purposes: to keep that particular task (e.g. running hospitals) clear of other tasks and uncontaminated; to entice high quality lay and professional leadership into public service; and to keep the task out of "politics."

This technique has less to recommend it than originally thought, because it is based on some naïve assumptions. "Politics" and the struggle for power, influence, privilege, and honor take place whatever the structure. It is perhaps a little more venal in some places than in others, but it goes on. Setting up somewhat separated, semi-autonomous bodies to carry out regular functions of government nurtures the all-too-vigorous tendencies toward competing empires. It limits the horizons of the people involved and makes it more difficult for them to see where they fit into the broad picture. It isolates a number of quality people from some of the less glamorous operations of city government and thus tacitly approves of "cheap politics," or at least cheaper politics, in those areas. It allows the responsible elected officials to diffuse their responsibility and thus their accountability before the public.

In matters concerning the ingredients of the slum problem, responsibility and authority for policy and action need to be at the nerve center. This nerve center must send and receive signals from all the relevant parts of the body—in this case, the decision makers (public officials and officers of enterprise), the agencies, the institutions that have some bearing on the slum problem, and the people of the slums themselves.

Since the slum problem is an integral part of the problem of the city, it does not make sense to think in terms of establishing an organization to cope with it. The organization is already there—the city government. It may be necessary to establish new pieces of machinery to fill out the mosaic of executive authority and competence, but in most cities the necessary agencies and departments exist. They need help to do things better and to relate to each other so they are more or less playing on the same team and heading in the same direction. The absence of such relationships has troubled more than one school principal who found his school unexpectedly inundated with new pupils because of urban renewal.

There certainly must be mechanisms for facilitating and encouraging communication and joint thinking among departments and agencies. It is doubtful that there is a favored pattern for this, except that communication, whatever it is, must take place at the highest levels of policy making as well as at the lower levels of operations and daily deciding.

The great danger of interdepartmental committees or coordinating councils is that they too are subject to powerful tendencies to relax into routine and inertia. It is wise, therefore, not to count on such devices always to produce driving action, profound analysis, and innovation. There is not any organizational structure per se that is going to produce these things. They depend on quality of leadership and the political and social atmosphere within which it is operating.

The eternal problem for political leaders and executives who want to improve the human condition is how to keep fresh breezes ventilating their administrative structures, legislatures, and bureaucracies. There is not any pat formula for this either. It helps, however, to let strangers look in once in a while. People from the academic world often are good at analyzing and criticizing and pointing out the inadequacies or irrelevancies in public or private operations. *Ad hoc* citizens groups checking on a particular aspect of city functioning sometimes come up with wise insights and suggestions. Inviting people from one guild to make critical observations of the operations of another guild may result in startling new perspectives and some shaking up. Teachers can comment on the welfare system, or social workers on public education. Physical planners can suggest to recreation people or police how they might do better. This sort of thing can be done occasionally or regularly.

The organizational problem is creating machinery to achieve and maintain executive vigor and consensus about objectives and strategy, machinery that is accessible to and eager for new knowledge and insights, and is capable of changing its ways.

Built-in capacity to change

Things do change and agencies and institutions need to make it possible for themselves to change, to keep up. There is nothing new about this thought, but there are certainly some new and different things that need to be done about it.

One of the things that impedes our ability to come to grips with the slum problem is the attachment of people and institutions to the way they do things now. Certain conditions used to exist and ideas about how to deal with these conditions also existed. Once upon a time someone established an organizational structure to carry out these ideas. The ideas were expressed in law or a charter or a constitution. A staff was hired, regulations were drawn up, offices were established, and away they went. Operations within this structure on the basis of its concepts and rules became a way of life for its personnel. This is the life history of most organizations, public or private.

The trouble is, conditions change, or new ideas and perceptions about how better to deal with the same conditions appear. What does the well-established organization do? History is not replete with inspiring examples of orderly institutional change to meet changing conditions or to utilize new knowledge. It almost seems that it cannot be done without a revolution or a palace revolution, or the old rascals being turned out and new ones put in, or a new organization being established to carry the ball.

This can be wasteful, too. A new municipal administration, for instance, may abandon existing policies, programs, and instrumentalities just *because* they are the products of the old administration and the new one has to make its own name and establish visible things that are identified with it alone.

What is needed is continuing or periodic objective assessment of existing policies and instrumentalities, the problems they are supposed to be affecting and the services they are providing.

There is no recipe for bringing about changes. All that can be said is that the idea of change must be kept respectable and rational change must be seen as desirable. Change is one aspect of the way things are these days, and we have to accept this with reference to social conditions as readily as we do for science.

The target is the city itself—
all of it, and its people

One other general thing should be said about policy and action designed to improve slum conditions. It is a serious error to think of the geography that is the slum as the only target or even the main target. Such a view implies that whatever is wrong is wrong with those people in that place; whatever surgery has to take place need take place only there. It is the deficiencies, imbalances, and shortcomings of the entire community that produce the slum conditions and that must, therefore, be the objective for corrective or preventive action. A change in the world outside the slum may make more of a difference inside than something introduced inside with the idea that change would result. For instance, a substantial increase in the payroll of a big employer of low-skilled workers would probably make more real difference in the slum than would the establishment in the area of a day care center or a child health clinic, important as those may be.

Another way of saying essentially the same thing is that indirect approaches are likely to have a greater pay-off than direct. Slum clearance, for example, will eliminate some physical manifestations of the slum problem, but it will not get at the causes, which by now all agree are not primarily connected with deteriorated real estate. Very often slum clearance simply has the effect of moving the slum somewhere else, or hastening the deterioration of another area to which the residents of the cleared slum are forced to move.

Division of labor

While keeping in mind the interconnectedness of all the aspects of slum life, and the interconnectedness of things to do about it, it is necessary to divide the subject of desirable policy and action in order to get hold of it and understand it. In execution it must be divided, too. As we have said before, there must be division of labor and departmentalization of effort. No complex organism could function if there were not. Therefore, we will talk about things to do in subjects that more or less fit the usual city structure and organization. The major headings are: education, economic self-sufficiency and employment, politics and citizen participation, the physical environment, social and health services, the arts.

CHAPTER III

Education

"MUCH AS disadvantaged children may try to hide their knowledge, they recognize full well that failure in education is terribly final, and for them spells the end of the American dream of progress through education." This quotation from the January 1963 report (page 1) of the Higher Horizons Program in New York City points to the first priority of education in any attack on slum problems.

Dr. James Bryant Conant says: "The improvement of slum conditions is only in part a question of improving education. But the role of the schools is of utmost importance." [1]

Robert Havighurst of the University of Chicago, an educator who has thought deeply about educational problems of the slums, said in an article in *New City:*

... we see the school as the main weapon to be used in improving the life chances of children born to inadequate families, but we see the school's effectiveness cut down through the existence of economic and racial segregation in our big cities. Social urban renewal is impossible without the active participation of educators and without some drastic changes in present-day educational programs.[2]

We have seen some facts about schools in the slums—high drop-out rates, low achievement scores, discipline problems, teacher turnover, low quality of teaching, small numbers of slum youth who go on to college, and inadequate financial investments in the inner city schools in comparison with the suburbs and outlying areas.

These are formidable things to change. The report of a 1962 conference at Columbia University stated that the outlook was "discouraging and hopeful. It is discouraging in terms of its size, complexity, bitterness, and the human cost involved. The outlook is hopeful in the forces which are being mobilized to dissect and resolve this wasteful, destructive problem of displaced citizens in a rejecting or ignoring homeland." [3] That change is of crucial importance cannot be denied.

Probably the most important mission of the schools in the slums is to convince slum children and youth that they are a part of America and can be successful. This sounds trite, but it points to the greatest deficiency in the schooling process in slum schools. The task of the schools is to provide the foundation upon which all can build the skills necessary to perform some remunerable economic function successfully. This means all—those who will be intellectuals and those who will move things around with their hands. This of course does not pretend to define the total role of the school, but merely emphasizes the special critical function of the school in low income areas.

Some things that need to be done for schooling in the

slums are fairly simple. It should be noted at this point that many of the things suggested are being done—some in one or two places, some in many places, nowhere adequately. Nowhere are they being done on a scale adequate to get ahead of the forces pushing back, much less to compensate for the cumulative depression of human capacity resulting from the years of inadequacy that have gone before. This is one of the ideas that must be accepted for a while in America. It is not enough just to bring schooling in the slums up to an average level. The level must be higher, if a dent is to be made. There must be a conscious policy, backed up by people, brains, and money, of *compensatory* education.

Even if nothing in slum schools is done differently than it is now, more teachers, more classrooms, more books, more equipment, more extra-curricular activities, more counselors are required. This presents difficult political and fiscal problems, but there is no point in deluding ourselves about the need just because the obstacles are formidable.

Early in 1964, Calvin E. Gross, Superintendent of Schools in New York City, proposed a program of "saturation" in the schools with low achievement rates. By this he did not mean necessarily providing new techniques and methods but rather applying adequate resources to these schools. Up to the present little has been done, but this was a public recognition by a school official that the slum schools need something extra.

John Kenneth Galbraith made a proposal in December, 1963, that attracted nationwide attention for its directness, simplicity, and relevance. He suggested that the hundred lowest income counties (or urban slums of similar population) in 1964 be designated as special educational districts. They would then be equipped with truly excellent and comprehensive school plants. Then, in the manner of the Peace Corps, an elite body of young teachers would be assembled ready to serve in the most difficult areas. Modest educational grants would be made to needy families to feed and clothe their children and compensate for their potential earnings. In the year following the next one hundred most abysmal areas would be selected, and so on. This Galbraith recommended as the most effective single step in the attack on poverty.

Reading

Probably the most important elements in schooling for slum children are reading and communications skills. This applies to the non-college bound as well as to the 20-40 per cent who will go to college. Without the ability to read (application forms, industrial instructions, health clinic forms, installment purchase contracts, legal summonses) nobody goes very far. Among the school population there is a 15-20 per cent reading inability. Among the educationally deprived this runs as high as 50 per cent.

This situation calls for a long list of actions. First, is just plain better teaching of reading along with remedial work for those who are already behind. Then comes better materials to read; books and papers that show the real life of the readers—including pictures of Negroes and Puerto Ricans and Mexicans and poor people; reading about subjects of immediate interest to the pupils—sports, their own neighborhoods, people they know, civil rights, and the like.

Starting to work on the cognitive skills and reading readiness of slum children before first grade or kindergarten age is essential. This is because youngsters from poor homes tend to be "culturally deprived." This means that they have not had much practice at conversation or hearing long sentences; they have little acquaintance with books; they are limited in experience and haven't been exposed to ideas much beyond the daily grubbing for existence. Such children enter school already far behind their middle class counterparts in their readiness to cope with those marks on the paper.

These pages do not attempt to go into the complex details of methods of teaching reading. There is vigorous debate on this subject and a layman in the field could easily be lost if he strayed too far into this forest, or he might be devoured by a voracious protagonist of one method or another. The New York State Department of Education holds that no one method is indispensable for teaching a child to read. A multiple approach should be used. The best methods are adapted to ability and achievement levels and to the nature of the group and of individuals. A child whose hearing is not acute may respond to visual methods. A child with defective vision will usually respond to the oral methods. The goal is not to teach children phonics, or the alphabet. The goal is to teach them to read.

The effective teaching of reading must be taken by the school as an objective of very high priority. The school cannot rest if significant numbers of its pupils are retarded in reading.

Community school

On a more general level is the idea of the community school. This holds promise of transforming the slum school from a headache for administrators, teachers, and pupils into a booster mechanism out of the slums. It is a simple idea, but like all the rest having to do with this subject, hard to work out and do it right. Also, like all the rest, if not done right it could turn into a monster and produce neither good education nor good community integration and service. Or, what is often even more depressing, it could just present a shell with no guts behind it. There has been a fair amount of talk about the community school in recent years. There are very few to be seen, and some of these are facade.

What is it? It is a place (the public school, or, in the case of Detroit, the school building and a community building on the same property) that attempts not only to educate the young through the usual methods of classes and teachers, but also to serve as a focal point for community activity, services, and concerns. This means not only providing space for meetings and affairs of the adults in the area, but also for services. The idea is that it become the hub of the community; that adults and children and youth alike see it and use it as a place that is theirs, has real meaning for them, and that they have a hand in running.

A community school is open all day and all night. The recreation department and other city agencies as well as community groups use it all the time. At night a wide range of classes or more informal approaches to education for adults take place. This is extended far beyond the usual adult education courses, although these have their place. Also included are efforts to make available basic information about the ways of the city (housing, police, welfare, and the like) to those who are often pushed around by these ways, but don't know much about the ins and outs. Many of the people in the slum are new to the city, or even if they have been there a while, they never have learned how to thread their way through the maze that is the urban environment.

Such a school is open the year round and provides a focal point for summer and weekend activities. It is a mistake to think that slum children will not sign up for summer school when a myriad of interesting things are offered. They will even sign up for remedial reading and arithmetic.

In such a place may be located a community worker to help residents of the area organize themselves for purposes ranging from purely social to civil rights, although the minute he starts doing things of this nature *for* the residents he might as well go somewhere else. The idea is for him to help them discover and organize to use their own independent strength to achieve the ends they see as important.

Also in the building are offices for appropriate public and private welfare services, for the public employment service, for a legal counselor to help people keep out of trouble (on such things as installment contracts) and to help see that their rights are protected when they do get into trouble with the law. This last is a vital function in a slum area, because the fact that our system of justice has not yet learned not to distinguish between those who have money and those who don't is a rankling and embittering and alienating force among the poor. Such a place should also have a room for the teenagers that they can run pretty much by themselves as a hangout, music hall, coffee house, place to air gripes and philosophy, and perform in their combos.

One threat to the essential idea of such a place is that it may be taken over as the exclusive domain of those residents who are already relatively highly motivated toward education and community activity. If this is allowed to happen, those who are timid, fearful, suspicious, outside, embarrassed about pushing themselves forward will be excluded, and they, after all, are the ones who most need to be encouraged and energized in positive directions.

The school is the right place for services and community activities for several reasons. First, it is located in the neighborhood. Elementary, junior high, and high schools are scattered all over all cities in the good areas and the bad. Second, since education is so crucial in deciding whether or not slum children will remain slum children, everything that supports and focuses on the educational process and helps to make it a vital part of life and not just something that has to be suffered is all to the good. Third, tradition says that the school belongs to everybody and is supposed to serve everybody. Community schools will make this more so.

Schools and parents

An aspect of a community school that is of prime importance and that can be developed whether or not the entire concept of the community school is adopted is the knitting together of the school, the parents, and other residents of the area.

Any number of studies have shown that children from low status families in low status neighborhoods do not get the support and push for education that youngsters in higher status areas do. The reasons for this are not very mysterious. Low status parents have themselves not had much education. This often results in a feeling of "What's good enough for me is good enough for my kid." In reality this may mask a feeling of embarrassment, resentment, and fear of the youngster's becoming "smarter" than the parent. Whatever the cause, it is an attitude which can only impede education. People in the slums are unable to see much evidence that they or their children are ever going to have a real chance at the high salary, high status jobs for which education is requisite. Therefore, why should the child waste his time staying in school any longer than the law says he has to, or why is it very important that he do well. This is a particularly potent negative force among Negroes who know full well that their color bars them from many opportunities, no matter how much education they get.

In a slum setting, the school is seen as the agent of a world that will not let you in. Your child has to go to school for a certain number of years, so you do not struggle against this. However, you do not help the process very much, and when he gets to the legal school leaving age you may very well encourage him to quit loafing, get out of school, and get a job. The school is authority over which you have no control. The school is "them." The trick is to make the school "us." How can it be done?

Some schools have hired people from the neighborhood, or recruited them as volunteers, to work with teachers and school social workers. Such a gesture says to the people in the neighborhood: "If they think enough of us to hire us, maybe it's not such a dumb place after all!" Such a person speaks the language of the neighborhood. This does not refer to words alone, but rather to the totality of communication. Such a person speaks in the language of the experience of that neighborhood and the people in it because he or she is one of them. This is a real bridge—a two-way bridge.

Some school personnel have functioned as community organizers themselves and have helped neighborhood groups to organize for better street lighting, to put on sports events, to run a clambake, to get police protection, to express themselves on an urban renewal plan they did not like.

Too often teachers in slum schools never see the inside of the homes of their charges, or if they do, it is only when Johnny is in trouble. Time for teachers to visit parents in their own homes, when they are there and when it is convenient for them (for some this is daytime, and for some it is night-time—Papa should be there, too) should be paid for by the Board of Education as a regular part of the teacher's duties. It may be as important as what goes on in the classroom.

Some new twists on the traditional American P.T.A. or Home and School Association need to be tried. A formal meeting with rules of procedure, speaker, question period, and coffee later may be quite unfamiliar and frightening to many people in the slums. They're just not used to this sort of thing. It is a more familiar pattern of life in suburbia. To be sure, all formality cannot be abandoned, but it need not be applied so universally and so unthinkingly. Some possible changes are smaller group discussions, different meeting times, baby sitting arrangements, less formal procedures, plans to send a friend to walk to the meeting with the new member, and discussion of things that really capture interest. These may make a difference and create an atmosphere in which communication can take place. School people in such groups should never forget that they have a lot to learn from the parents. This attitude alone, if genuine, may be as important as anything else in breaking the silence barrier between school and the parent with little formal education.

Tutoring

Another person who can do a lot for the youngsters in the slum school, as well as for the atmosphere of the neighborhood, is the tutor or homework helper. Successful high-school juniors or seniors can help elementary pupils with their school work. The tutors or helpers can themselves be youngsters from low-income families, preferably from the same neighborhoods as the pupils.

Tutoring does several things. It helps the elementary pupils who are falling behind or having a hard time. It rewards the successful high-school students. It sets up the boy or girl who does well in his school work as a desirable model for youngsters, who then can see that academic success does bring rewards. It gives high status and encouragement to the tutors to continue to do well and to continue their education beyond high school. It tells the parents that good work in school means something and that the school is willing to recognize the quality of their own children. It gives parents and children alike a new reason to hope about the future and a little more reason to leave behind the fatalism and "live for the present" attitude of so many low status people. When you have some hope that things can be better in the future, you start doing things to prepare for it.

These are not the only kinds of tutors that can be helpful in a school in a low income area. Volunteer students from a nearby college, high-school students from better areas, and adult volunteers can all pitch in. They can tutor individually, help with homework in small groups, and supervise evening study halls. They are valuable resources too seldom exploited.

Wider horizons

In addition to exerting extra effort within the slum schools and in their immediate environs, the school must also widen horizons for pupils. The fact that many slum children have never been exposed to some common city experiences never fails to shock the interested observer. In New York a child may never see the United Nations, or even hear of it. In Chicago it may be the lake front that is unknown. In New Orleans, the zoo. The horizons of many, many slum children are extremely limited. They may know a great deal about a number of things the middle class child knows little about: sex, the police, drunks, gang fights, family brawls, and the like. But they know little about the city beyond their own neighborhood, the city government, offices and factories and hospitals, and the city's cultural resources. Some more intimate knowledge of the world beyond the neighborhood can help the youngster to make it over the hurdles his life has put in his way. The slum school should make familiarization with the city and its opportunities a routine part of its schedule.

Team teaching

Two modifications of the usual school organization and methods may have greater relevance in the slum school than elsewhere, although they are valid anywhere. These are team teaching and the ungraded primary.

Team teaching groups three to six teachers with complementary skills and a teaching aide and clerk under one more experienced teacher as the leader. They function as a unit with as many pupils as would be handled by the same number of teachers if they each had a separate class. With the team teaching system, however, it is possible to organize the pupils in groups of varying sizes at different times, depending on what is to be done. The whole group can be assembled at one time with one teacher, while the other teachers may be working with individual pupils for special or remedial work. At other times several groups of varying size may be doing different things.

This system allows for different patterns for different needs; provides more opportunity for special work with individuals or very small groups who need it (because they are ahead or behind); allows for close supervision of the newer or less qualified teachers (often the majority in the less desirable schools in poor areas); permits more efficient use of equipment and space in the school, both of which are usually at a premium in slum schools; relieves the teacher of many clerical tasks. In other words, team teaching tends to make for better teaching, and in view of the greater educational deficiencies of slum children, better teaching is an urgent need.

Ungraded primary

The ungraded primary organizes the first several years without the labels of first, second, and third grade. This makes for greater flexibility in meeting the widely varying needs and levels of progress of children in the earliest years of school. Under this system, it is easier for the teacher to accommodate himself to the drags and spurts of the child. He can work intensively over a long period of time with children who have had little brain stimulation without having to hold them back in one grade when their friends are moving up. Thus there is a better chance of avoiding the beginning of the succession of failures that is the school experience for so many and imprinting the self image of failure in the mind of the child at so early a stage in his career.

Teachers

Teachers in slum schools are generally not as well qualified as those in better areas. There are two reasons for this: slum schools are hardship posts and teachers generally prefer to teach in "nicer" places with "nicer" children; and teachers are not trained for the special problems of slum schools nor helped to adjust to a culture and value system very different from what most of them are used to.

Slum schools are difficult and will be for a long time. They are truly hardship posts. They are usually in old buildings, inadequately equipped and supplied, overcrowded, and in dirty and dangerous neighborhoods. They present heartbreaking educational and disciplinary problems. Some dedicated teachers would not work anywhere else because they see the challenge and they have seen the changes that can be made. But the majority would rather teach in the schools in the wealthier neighborhoods, and who can blame them! Teachers in slum schools should be given a bonus, either monetary or in service credit. How can we define a slum school for this purpose? In a high school, the standard could be the drop-out rate, in elementary school, the reading scores. It does not take much more than that to tell what's what.

The second important aspect of the question of teaching personnel is more difficult to define and perhaps more difficult to remedy. Most teachers come from middle class backgrounds.

Most of the people in the slums are lower class. About 75 per cent of public school teachers can be identified as middle class. As has been pointed out earlier, lower class, or lower status people usually look at things differently than middle class people. Why shouldn't they? They are looking up from down there. They think certain things are worthwhile and others not. These are not always the same things valued by people from the middle class.

It is easy to see how such a situation can make for difficulty in communication, in understanding and acceptance between teacher and pupil and teacher and parent. Without this, the skids for the learning process are not going to be very well greased. There probably is no complete answer to this problem because real communication and mutual acceptance across social class lines is extraordinarily difficult to achieve, particularly where adults are involved. This is easy enough to understand. There is a simple old saying: Birds of a feather flock together. And these are not the same kind of bird. That is all there is to it.

But this is no reason to despair, because the effects of these differences in outlook can be ameliorated in the relationship between teacher and pupil. It is important that strenuous efforts be made to ameliorate them, because slum children must have a feeling that middle class people are not only worthwhile and that their position is worth striving for, but also that middle class people are not so bad after all, that they are understanding and accepting and helpful and hospitable and would be glad to see a lower class person make it to the middle class.

This statement opens the way for the rhetorical question: Are you trying to make nice little middle class boys and girls out of lower class children? Yes, for some, no for others. This is where the matter of free choice comes in again. The goal is to make it possible for those with the inherent capacity, strength, drive, and intelligence to make it to middle class income and way of life if they so choose. This is the desirable status in America, no matter how you cut it. This does not say that all the attributes and values of middle class life in America are exemplary. They are not. One has only to read any popular magazine to find this out. But changing these is another subject. Robert Weaver, Administrator of the Housing and Home Finance Agency, stated the dual goal clearly.

> Perhaps our first objective must be to find techniques for assisting the transition to middle class status of those who are obviously upwardly mobile. For non-whites, for example, this will mean intensified efforts to increase opportunities for training and education which will enable them to enter professional, technical, and managerial groups. It will mean a continued struggle against discrimination in employment. And, as I have mentioned earlier, it will require that racial bars in housing and residence be removed.
>
> The second objective involves the more difficult task of finding ways to "accelerate the effective functioning in urban life of those who do not become middle class." Accepting such an objective may be difficult because it will require us to modify some of our traditional optimistic assumptions both about the availability of middle class rewards in our society and about the ability of individuals whose experiences or expectations have been devoid of middle class rewards to respond to them quickly.[4]

Middle class teachers can be helped to perform better in slum schools. Some of their training should be in slum schools and they should get a heavy dose of the sociology, politics, and economics of the slums in their curriculum. The same thing should be done for teachers already in service. An effort should be made to recruit new teachers from low income areas. These are people who can understand and connect with the culture of the underprivileged because they have had inside experience. There is danger in this because often a person who has "made it" up the ladder from his lowly beginnings does not want to look back. He may even be more hostile toward those on his former level than someone who has never had the experience. He does not want to be reminded that he was not born with a silver spoon in his mouth. This danger does not argue against the idea of recruiting teachers from low income backgrounds, however. It is just something to watch for.

School and work experience

Work experience during the school years can be a valuable learning and motivating device. This is applicable at any place in society (witness the successful devotion of Antioch College to the systematic combination of work and schooling) but it is particularly relevant in the lives of slum youngsters. In the words of the Phi Delta Kappa education fraternity, the purpose of work-study programs is "to prevent certain youngsters from becoming alienated from their society." [5]

Because so many slum youngsters drop out before finishing high school, it is important that every effort be made to prepare them for moving from school into a job before they have escaped. In fact, good work-study programs seem to have a double effect. They help to prepare the youngster for the world of work before he is thrown into it on his own, and at the same time they exert a subtle pressure on the boy or girl to stay in school. The reason for this is that pupils begin to learn first hand the practical value of education.

In 1961, there were work-study programs of one kind or another in about 1,500 school districts across the country. In 1957, DeWitt Hunt listed criteria that work-study programs should meet before they could be dignified as part of an educational process:

> The student performs socially useful tasks at a level of proficiency commensurate with his own highest ability; the work performed is supervised by a qualified school official; school credit for the work is based on both qualitative and quantitative judgments of the work done, and is granted toward high school graduation; it thus becomes part of the student's personnel record; the work experience for credit must be gained during school-released time; the student may or may not receive remuneration for the work done; the coordinator or supervisor should meet the students enrolled in the work experience program in a special class in which problems of public relations and job success are considered; local, state, and federal labor laws and regulations pertaining to the employment of youth are observed; care is taken that no exploitation of student labor results; the controlling purposes of work experience programs may range from guidance and general education to vocational education for a specific occupation.[6]

The Phi Delta Kappa Commission on the Role of the School in the Prevention of Juvenile Delinquency added a few more criteria.

> . . . it will commence at age thirteen or fourteen and continue to age eighteen, though many boys will graduate from it a year or two before age eighteen; it will attempt to teach boys elementary work disciplines: punctuality, ability to take orders

from a boss, ability to work cooperatively with others in a team, responsibility on the job; it will lead directly into stable adult jobs; it will be part of the public school program, with the curriculum adapted to the intellectual level, the interest in practical endeavors, and the work-experience program of alienated youth.[7]

Some of these criteria might be considered not absolutely necessary for a legitimate school-sponsored work-study program, but they set up a goal, and they reveal what the idea is all about.

In summary, a work-study program begins to open the youngster's eyes to what lies beyond school; it eases the transition from school to work (which is never effectively made by many drop-outs without help); it begins to teach the youngster what wage work is and what are its rules; it persuades many that perhaps they had better stay in school longer than they had planned. For those whose minds and spirits, if not yet their bodies, have abandoned school, it provides a new system to be identified with and to see a future in.

The male image

Another thing to keep in mind about large numbers of slum youngsters, particularly Negroes, is that their families often are not headed by men. Earlier it has been pointed out that a common characteristic among lower status families is that the pilot of the family is a woman: mother, grandmother, aunt, or older sister, make it a "female based family." There is a big and important gap in the lives of boys and girls in such situations.

The prescription is immediately apparent: more men teachers in slum schools for the youngsters to know, admire, look up to, identify with, and be disciplined by. Volunteer men can also help with extra curricular activities, sports and the like.

Scholarships

A good solid scholarship program for high school students in slum schools would make a difference. Scholarships would go to juniors and seniors with academic potential, even some sophomores should be helped. Scholarships would be awarded by a committee of the school faculty with perhaps the participation of a few citizens from the area and a representative of a college or university in the community. The scholarships might require some work on the part of the recipient. Their purpose would be manifold: to propel the capable student toward education beyond the high school; to reward good work in school in an environment where this is not always highly valued; to reduce economic pressures to drop out; to introduce the strange idea of the scholarship to the slum school (relatively few scholarships go to students in low income lower class areas); to demonstrate to the community and its unbelieving institutions that there is academic potential in the slum school although it takes some mining to get it.

Kansas City, Missouri, has pioneered with a supportive program for promising students in high schools in low income areas. This involves scholarship aid during part of the high school years, extra effort in guidance and moral support, and facilitation of access to college scholarships. Kansas City is even contemplating starting some aspects of the program at the junior high-school level.

Older youth

The school should accept more responsibility for youth between the ages of sixteen and twenty-one, particularly in the slums. With rare exceptions, the age of sixteen signals the end of all relationships between school and youth in low income areas, and yet it is apparent that many youngsters are far from ready to be dumped on their own on an unfriendly labor market at that age. An aggressively helpful posture on the part of the high-school districts in the inner city might be a decisive factor in what happens to many older youth who left school before graduation, and even many who have graduated but are still having a hard time on their own.

This means utilizing many communication devices, such as circulars, newspaper ads, posters, radio and television announcements, and word of mouth, people, such as detached workers, and places, such as bars, cafes, and pool halls. All these will help to get the word out that the school still has something for you even if you are eighteen and have dropped out before finishing: help with job placement, more training either in an occupational skill or just plain basic education, and counseling. The school must be prepared to provide these things on a flexible basis and with whatever timing and location of classes and individual counseling best suits the situation. Some of the counseling and perhaps some classes might take place outside the school building.

Although by this time many boys of eighteen have awakened to the fact that they need more training, education, and help in getting a job, there may still be a reluctance to go back to the school building itself, which is not a place they remember with much pleasure. Fire stations, libraries, fraternal lodges, union halls, and other public and semi-public buildings could be used for some of these services.

The pupil mix: social class

One of the important things about a school in the inner city is the pupil mix. Professor Robert Havighurst [8] of the University of Chicago lays great stress on this and its relevance to what takes place in the educational process, as well as how it affects the whole character of the inner city. It is generally accepted as a desirable objective that inner city districts should be more heterogeneous than they now are in race, income level, and social class. Income or ethnic ghettoes within the city are not healthy.

Although many forces tend toward the creation and perpetuation of ghettoes, one of the more potent is the quality and character of public school education. Many middle class families who otherwise would like to stay in the city feel impelled to move to the suburbs to get better education for their children. They want their children to be equipped to go on to college and feel that many of the schools in the inner city will not do this as well as those in the suburbs. And they are right.

In addition, though they may not be familiar with the scientific evidence that proves it, they feel in their bones that their middle class child will do less well in a school which is dominated numerically by lower class children. The child of a working class family will do better if he is one of a minority of working class children in a middle class school than he will if he is one of a majority of working class children in a working class school. The quality of performance of children in school depends on the socioeconomic character of the school, independent of the socioeconomic status of the child.[9] Therefore the prescription is: Do not let a school become overwhelmingly populated by the noncollege-bound or dominated by pupils from deprived backgrounds. This is admittedly difficult, but important.

Havighurst points out that in reality, for some time to come, elementary schools will tend to be segregated by economic status of families, since elementary school districts are small and cannot have much socioeconomic variety. Secondary schools now tend to be segregated by ability levels and occupational goals. His recommendation is that at least for a transition period while "social urban renewal" is under way, a college-preparatory high school with good academic standards needs to be available to all areas of the city. Such a school should have a mixed socioeconomic and race composition. He recognizes that this means sacrificing the traditional American educator's belief that one and only one high school should serve all the children of a given geographical district. This simply is not possible under present conditions, if the best educational resources are going to be available in the inner city for the children of those families with academic aspirations. "The principal obstacle to social urban renewal at present is the high school with fixed geographical boundaries which becomes dominated by lower class children who do not have academic ambitions." [10]

His conclusion is that the best policy, at least during a transition period, is to establish one or more academic high schools in a local community, admitting students liberally (the top 50 per cent in school grades and academic ability).

The academic school would be supplemented with one or more schools that explicitly have other functions, such as a good commercial or vocational high school, and a unit to provide work experience under school supervision for pupils who are almost certain to drop out upon reaching the legal school leaving age.

The pupil mix: color

Akin to the question of social class mix is that of color mix, although this is obviously much more of a political and civic hot potato. Segregated schooling is poor schooling. This principle is now imbedded in the law of the land and accepted by those who are not blinded by their own fear and inadequacy

We have seen, aside from the feelings of injustice, unfairness, and pessimism that pervade a segregated situation and have a discouraging effect on the educational process, that the segregated group is a culturally more limited group because of its history. This too has a depressing effect on the way schooling "takes." Some may validly argue that an all-Negro school is more comfortable and less threatening for the pupils since they do not have to compete with white pupils who, on the average, already have an advantage over the Negroes because of the higher educational level of their families. This may be true in some cases. On the other hand, it is probably as valid to argue that competition with white pupils may pep up the Negro students because they are under the challenge to "show" the whites.

Whichever the case, the argument is irrelevant. Segregated education as a matter of policy is finished in this country. It yet remains to desegregate in fact, and this will take time because of the complexity of the factors involved. However, as this is written so many things are happening on the racial front that no one can be sure what the situation will be next week.

Because of the complexity and the power of the factors that have produced and now conspire to maintain racial segregation, the schools themselves cannot change the pattern immediately. This is not meant to relieve them of the responsibility to try, however. It is merely to say that while they should try hard to get a racial mix in the schools, it is equally important for under-privileged Negro pupils to get strong compensatory education. The fact that a board of education is seriously attempting to overcome *de facto* segregation, even though it does not magically achieve full success, will have a heartening effect in the Negro community. This will help to avoid some of the tension and fights that can take place around the issue of segregated schools and reserve this energy for common attack on some of the problems that are so difficult to solve even with good will on all sides.

Let it quickly be said that there is nothing wrong with a good fight. It certainly has energizing and mobilizing effects and is often better adult education than what takes place in the classroom under that label. A fight across racial lines is not a good thing, however.

There are several approaches to reducing segregation in schools aside from basic changes in residential patterns. One is site selection for new schools. New sites have to be chosen in accord with a long list of criteria. One of the important criteria should be the color composition of the area and the potential student body. It should be as heterogeneous as possible. The problem here is that residential patterns change with the changing city, and a heterogeneous school this year may be all black or all white five years from now.

Another criterion is redistricting. It is a fact that our cities are cross-hatched with school district lines drawn with the objective of maintaining *de facto* school segregation. This should be faced and district lines redrawn within the limits of feasibility. This, again, is no panacea. Residential patterns will continue to change, and what do you do with a district deep inside a Negro ghetto? There is not much that can be done about redrawing such a district's boundary lines so that some white pupils would attend the schools.

Redistricting, like anything having to do with this issue, engenders a lot of heat. Henry Saltzman had this to say:

> The issue of gerrymandering school districts is very much alive, and I sense a growing inclination on the part of school superintendents to want to see this one settled in the court. Because of the emotionalism—white and Negro—generated around rezoning, perhaps it is only from the Bench that a reasonable perspective can be obtained. This is not a pleasant prospect to most administrators. It may not be the only alternative. Recent events in San Francisco and Oakland indicate that where the Board of Education goes into active partnership with Negro leadership around these issues, and *is willing to recognize, frankly and openly, race as a consideration,* legal redress may be postponed, or, hopefully, made unnecessary.[11]

Open enrollment or "bussing" is a factor. This is a policy that allows a child to go to a school outside of his normal district. Sometimes this may be based on transfer to an underutilized school from an overcrowded one. Sometimes, as in Philadelphia, there may be reasons other than overcrowding for accepting an application for transfer. This implies that there is racial concentration, but does not actually say so. In New York City, the open enrollment policy has been explicitly and openly directed at racial imbalance. Schools that are 90 per cent or more homogeneous by race are designated as sending schools. All schools with vacancies are listed and parents of children in the sending schools can choose from this list the receiving schools they prefer. Transportation is provided free by the Board of Education (which is not the case in all cities with open enrollment policies).

Again, this is no panacea, and may even have some negative side effects, such as inconvenience and the fact that the child's fellow pupils are not likely to be his playmates after school back in his own neighborhood.

Integration of faculties is important. This means Negro teachers in all or predominantly white schools, and vice versa, although the former is more important. For many white children and their parents, working with a Negro teacher may represent their first experience in meeting a non-white who is their peer culturally, educationally, and economically. This can have subtle and far-reaching effects on racial attitudes. One of the realities of white pupil, parent, and teacher reaction in an integrated school is that the whites are shocked and put off by the behavior and academic performance of the Negro pupils who are probably predominantly lower class, even in suburban schools. Just because the pupils are physically mixed in the school does not mean there are necessarily real friendship ties among them.

The "educational park" of which Max Wolff is perhaps the leading proponent is an interesting idea for the big city. An educational park is, or rather would be, since there is not yet any such thing in a large urban center, a collection of educational facilities and buildings serving pupils from a large geographical area, from kindergarten through high school or even college. This gets away from the neighborhood school concept, which almost guarantees *de facto* segregated schools where residential patterns follow color lines. An educational park would be a place of good education, or at least education of uniform standards, for pupils of many different ethnic backgrounds and social positions since the net which would be cast over a large urban district would catch all kinds. Aside from this major objective, substantial economies in physical facilities would be possible as well as better supervision and in-service training of teachers. The principal drawbacks would be the transportation of small children long distances to the school and the difficulties of establishing close relations between teachers and parents. The case is not yet clear that the educational park would be good for the big city. It has enough in its favor, however, to warrant careful analysis.

All of these techniques to foster integration in schools should be used. At the same time, it must be recognized that none of them can be completely effective, nor can a board of education accomplish desegregation by itself. Saltzman summed up the real target this way: "For large-scale societal integration at the level of the employment market, schools will have to compensate for the educational deficiencies of deprived children, in the process facing the issue of spending more money per child in the slums and grey areas than in the middle-class neighborhoods." [12]

Programmed instruction and teaching machines

Teaching machines operate on the basis of self-instruction over a course of study that is laid out (programmed) and controlled by the learner at his own speed. Some recent experiments indicate that these machines may be useful for pupils of limited educational achievement. For one thing, they are interesting gadgets to play with. The pace of instruction can be controlled by the learner himself. There is no public embarrassment when the pupil gets an answer wrong. He is competing only with himself. There is immediate reinforcement and constant encouragement to keep going. This ties in with the "present time orientation" of lower class people. In this case, instead of waiting several days for the results of taking a test, the pupil sees the question and answer process simultaneously. If the answer is correct, he knows it immediately. If it is wrong, he learns immediately what the right answer is. There is no reason to cheat.

More trials should be undertaken with programmed instruction in slum schools. Experience so far is good enough to warrant further development.

Obviously, teaching machines are but one of a number of teaching aids. Over-reliance must not be placed on them. They are useful but can never replace the human warmth and understanding of a good teacher. They provide a certain kind of motivation, but not necessarily the strongest and most lasting kind.

Year-round schools

Time is too precious for the summer months to be lost from formal education. It is expensive to keep public schools open in the summer, but, given the ground that needs to be made up in slum areas, this is an expense that is of relatively little moment. Experience shows that if the schools were open for voluntary enrollment in low income, urban areas, they would be full of children. The program could be made somewhat more informal than that of the regular school year, but academic content need not be sacrificed to this to too great a degree. Remedial work should be offered, as well as advanced work for academically successful students.

A word about books

It is easy for a well-educated person to be overly sentimental about books. It is perhaps easier to underestimate the importance of books in upgrading levels of education, knowledge, and understanding. Slum schools must do much better in promoting the use of books, making them easily available, giving some away.

A lot of insight and information gets passed along through the written word; connections with the larger world and with humankind and its ideas are made vibrant and dramatic. Books provide rich emotional experience for many youngsters, once they can read the words with facility and come to regard books as a part of their environment. Books are a symbol of and a guide to human advancement. A child who owns a few books owns more than paper, cardboard, and ink.

Slum schools should have books in classrooms. They should

have good libraries, and should encourage the youngsters to use them. They should let pupils take books home and should be fully prepared to lose a few. If the public library system is not alert to its opportunities in slum areas, school people should take the librarians by the hand and lead the way toward introducing books into the lives of slum people by every imaginable device of promotion and distribution.

The preceding pages have touched on some ways to improve education in slum areas. It is worth repeating the conviction that the public education system could be the most important single channel through which significant and lasting changes in slum conditions can be brought about over the years.

Is this asking too much of the school? No. The public school as an institution is seen by many thoughtful people as the agent for passing on the rules and regulations and values and mores of a culture to its initiates. It is not seen as an agent of change. If the society of which it is a part changes, then the school will change also and pass along the new rules. The schools in Cuba are one of the most recent examples of this. Their curriculum has been totally changed in order to transmit new messages.

In this context, it is not so much a matter of asking the public school to initiate change, but rather to respond, along with other institutions, to the *necessity* for change as articulated by civic and political leadership and to adjust its methods accordingly. The school is not an exclusive instrument and cannot be viewed and used in isolation. It is not run by a coterie of experts who have the "word."

The school must mesh its efforts with other forces affecting or operating in the slum area if its full potential for influencing human development is to be approached. Among these forces is political leadership.

It must not be forgotten that the schools cannot do an an adequate job of preparing young people for independent productive life if the objective opportunities for independent productive life are in short supply. You cannot have an independent productive life if you do not have a job with an adequate income.

In *Slums and Suburbs,* Dr. Conant stressed this as he reviewed the problems of schools in slums and suburban areas. The final paragraph of the book states: "To improve the work of the slum schools requires an improvement in the lives of the families who inhabit the slums, but without a drastic change in the employment prospects for urban Negro youth, relatively little can be accomplished." [13]

S. M. Miller also emphasizes this theme:

If job opportunities are improved, then perhaps in the next generation a greater number of the children of the new working classes may make real moves to improve their conditions. It is not sufficiently realized that former disprivileged ethnic groups did not improve their conditions mainly by education, but through assimilation by business and political employments. The Irish and Italians did not initially have a heavy emphasis on education as vehicles for improvements. It was usually after the parents had made some economic stake—frequently through business—that Irish and Italian youth began to go to college. The Jews were different in that more of their ascent was through education; the emphasis on literacy and learning among Jews has been noted as important in their movement. Ignored has been the fact that in the "old country" many of them were petty traders and small business men so that they came to this nation with more varied experience than do the new working classes of today. Moreover, the Jew, like many other ascending ethnics, but unlike Negroes and Puerto Ricans, has religious values which maintained male importance and family solidarity.[14]

This paragraph is an important summary of the situation of today's slum dwellers. Miller would not endorse the position of first importance given to education in the preceding pages. It is not necessary, however, to get into this chicken and egg argument. He would probably not disagree with any of the specific suggestions that have been made concerning what needs to be done in slum schools. Policy and action directed to the slum problem must encompass many fronts at the same time. It is not a question of concentrating on increasing job opportunities first and then working to improve education in the slums, or vice versa. If both (and a lot of other things) do not move forward at the same time, each aspect will be less effective.

Miller's view on this is strong and clear, and has much to support it if one falls into the trap of advocating one arena or another as the exclusive or even dominant place to locate the action. He is worth quoting further, since he raises an issue of great importance:

In American life, it has been customary to offer "education" as the panacea for all problems, whether those of racial prejudice, sexual happiness or economic conflict. I have the feeling that to the problems of discrimination, inadequate economic functioning and poverty, we are again offering the reply of "education." In doing so we are essentially making it a bootstrap operation, telling those who have the most strikes against them, that they have to do the most work to improve the situation. I am saying that schools and education cannot be *expected* to solve the blight of poverty and inhumanity—the entire society and economy are implicated. And, it may be, that by our stress on eliminating drop outs we are not politicalizing the important issues. At the same time, we may be giving people a comfortable way to forget about the corrosive character of much of our social and economic life.[15]

CHAPTER IV

Economic
Self-Sufficiency
and Employment

S LUM CONDITIONS are not going to improve unless slum
dwellers (those who have not yet been destroyed) have
opportunities to work and to have income sufficient to support at least modest aspirations for betterment and for personal
growth. Those who cannot work because of age or physical or
mental incapacity must be supported by money and necessary
services so they do not have to rot away their remaining years
in infectious squalor.

There are two sides of this question of working and earning
money: opportunity and personal capacity. Also involved are
the linking mechanisms between job and job seeker.

Involved in this subject are some very big and complex
national and international economic questions. No one person
can deal with all these questions in depth. It is worth noting
that this example of limitations on the knowledge of any individual is one of the vexing problems of modern society.

Knowledge in many fields is increasing at an overwhelming pace. Conditions and events in one sphere of human activity more and more vitally affect other spheres, and yet it is increasingly difficult for people concerned with the broad spectra of human affairs even to be superficially acquainted with new knowledge in fields outside their own.

This situation is directly relevant to the shaping of policy and action on slums, because slum conditions are the product of so many interlacing forces. The educator may overemphasize educational prescriptions, perhaps without full awareness of changes in the society or the economy that make some of them irrelevant. The city planner may make rational and systematic plans that are thrown completely out of kilter by social forces of which his training and previous experience did not make him aware. The economist may recommend public policies that will increase the tax base for the local government and stimulate the development of new industry or services, only to find special interests blocking the way. *Meshing the knowledge of all relevant fields for concerted and consistent policy and action is a prime objective of movers and shakers whose interest is the slum.*

The man who sits on a hot spot more than anyone else is the mayor. He is accompanied sometimes by the county supervisor, the superintendent of schools, citizen members of boards and committees, but the bottoms of none of them are as uncomfortable as that of the mayor, who has to balance out the elements of the grand equation at the point of highest pressure—the city.

If his responses are narrow, if they are foreshortened by the perspective of his own term in office or an impending election, if they are not based on the knowledge and insights of all seven of the blind men feeling the elephant, he is likely to be remembered in one of two ways: as the man who was irrelevant in the lives of the majority of his constituents, or as the man whose political career was ended because he failed to comprehend the many facets of the organism for which he asked and received responsibility.

There are obviously crucial elements in the slum equation that are beyond the reach of local manipulators. Without a busy national economy with a steady growth rate (less sluggish than it is as this is written); without substantially less general unemployment than the 5-6 per cent that has been the case in recent years; without high productivity and fuller use of existing plant capacity; without expanding national and international markets, it is difficult to be optimistic about how much the low levels of human living that characterize the slums can be raised. The economy must be such that the private sector demands workers with a wide range of skills. In addition to this, the federal government must have the resources, drawn from the workings of a dynamic economy, to underwrite or directly stimulate the employment of the marginal workers the economy does not utilize.

A vigorous economy must provide the matrix within which the special economic situation of slum dwellers can be improved.

Adequate wages

Those who are employed in the private sector of the economy must be paid *wages high enough* to enable them to support a good standard of living for themselves and their families, and beyond that to "recapitalize" their families where they have stagnated or deteriorated because of past lack of investment. This means investment in education, in health, in broadening horizons through travel and exploitation of the cultural resources of the city. A low wage policy affecting large numbers of workers is restrictive and regressive. It prevents the development of individuals as producers as well as consumers. A *sine qua non* of a fast-moving economy is strong and widely distributed purchasing power. Great numbers of people can get this only out of the economy itself, in the form of wages, salaries, and returns on investments. Wages are the strongest contributor to the bulk of active purchasing power simply because there are more people who get wages. If certain sectors of the economy are unwilling or unable to follow a high wage policy or if trade union organization is not strong enough to force it, there is a legitimate role for minimum wage legislation with higher minimums and wider coverage.

Guaranteed minimum income

For those below the minimum income, a *guaranteed minimum income* should be established and administered by the federal government. This could be done by a sort of reverse income tax. Everyone would report his income. If it falls below a certain level, and is attested to be below that level in the current year as well, he receives payments to make up the difference between his income and the established minimum decent income level. This does not do violence to any principle in the American ethic. Public relief is now available to certain categories of people whose income falls below specified levels. However, it is hit or miss around the country, limited to certain categories (the aged, families of dependent children, and the like), and generally inadequate in terms of its stated purpose of providing temporary assistance to enable needy people to live and be well and to grow. The "means test" is applied to every case. It costs a tremendous amount of money to administer and is thoroughly degrading to the applicant. It is one more insult added to those life has already handed him. Every applicant has to prove that he or she is poor and be checked up on. Why shouldn't it be handled just like the income tax? Just check up on some of them.

Parity payments to farmers are based on a similar principle. The difference here is that these payments tend to go to people who as a group have political power and who are fairly well off. And while farmers are respectable, the poor are punished for being poor.

Some things that would lead to increased opportunities for employment for less advantaged, less skilled, less motivated, less educated, less monied people are discussed in the following sections.

Non-discriminatory employment policies

It is much clearer to many more people now than it was a year or two back that such policies are essential if we are to have harmony in our cities and our country. When Negroes, Puerto Ricans, and Mexicans have access to jobs equal with that of other members of the community, a prime depressant of their status, level of living, and ultimately their capacity will have been removed.

Accent on youth

There are never unlimited resources to apply to any given problem in the city and therefore hard choices must be made about priorities. Although no aspect of the employment picture should be ignored, there is a strong case for giving high priority to efforts to develop employment opportunities for younger workers (late teens and early twenties). Making such an allocation will be extremely difficult, since there are strong arguments the other way, too, and vocal supporters of the view that breadwinners and older workers come first. The unions are likely to be in this chorus.

There are several arguments for giving high priority to younger job seekers. Many of them are already breadwinners and the rewards for starting young families on a stable economic base is evident, when the pressures toward discouragement, surrender, and family breakup are weighed in the balance. Even if he has not yet established a family, it is of transcendent importance that the young man get connected with the world of work. He must avoid the diseases of disconnection, alienation, disaffection, down-spiraling, and crystalization of failure. From the point of view of commerce and industry, the younger workers are likely to be more responsive to modern industrial training. Younger people getting jobs rather than being forced into aimlessness by lack of opportunity will give a sense of optimism to those around them, which in itself will have an invigorating effect.

An accent on youth requires a whole range of specific policies and actions. It is at the junior high school level (grades eight and nine or ages twelve to fourteen) that the first conscious focus on employment should come, although, hopefully, realistic general information about occupations and the way people earn their livings will have been given to children in elementary school. Ignorance of occupations among the poor is widespread.

At the junior high-school level, a more systematic and conscious effort to teach youngsters the realities of the world of work is of great importance. This effort should include all the useful teaching devices: readings, films, classroom projects, speakers from representative occupations, and visits to places where people work. For some, whose experience with the traditional school pattern is proving to be nothing but failure and misery, a working experience (usually in a group) can be introduced as part of schooling. Care must be taken that a program of work experience in junior high school, with its necessary companion of modification (simplification) of academic curriculum, not guarantee that the youngster involved never gets a regular high school diploma or goes on to post high school education.

In the high school years, similar kinds of things can be done, with greater emphasis on individual jobs and relating curriculum to job. Occupational counseling in high school needs to be much strengthened. A frequent complaint from school people, employment service people, and informed outsiders, is that run-of-the-mill counselors in high schools are not well enough informed about the labor market, changing skill requirements, occupations with growth potential, and the like. This is undoubtedly unfair to many counselors who work hard to keep themselves informed, but as a generality is not far off the mark. Much can be done to make the public employment services more effective in connecting young people with work. Changes in this direction are taking place, but slowly. Traditionally the public employment service has sought to find the best qualified person to fill whatever job vacancies are listed. No one can take issue with this, but it does not meet the needs of the hard to place, among which are youth, and particularly youth from the slums.

To meet their needs, the employment services in some forward-looking states (notably California) have moved right into the high school. Not just in the building after school hours, but during the school day. The employment service helps the school with job counseling and testing and does some placement. This can be done to a lesser degree in churches, lodge halls, community centers, settlement houses, and other buildings in the slum neighborhoods where the footloose, jobless, unskilled youth can be found. New York state has experimented with this somewhat. But probably most important is a close operational connection between the school and the employment service.

At least one big-city school system has tried to take more aggressive responsibility for out-of-school youth up to the age of twenty-one. A Chicago school district attempted with moderate success to take a census of all youth up to age twenty-one in the district who were out of school and out of work. Through letters, word of mouth, contact with parents, and so on, contact was established with the youth and help offered them in job placement, getting back into some kind of formal education, and counseling.

The Mobilization for Youth program in New York City established the Youth Jobs Center to perform the function of linking youth with jobs, counseling, brief training in basic skills, such as filling out applications and dressing properly. In San Francisco, the Youth Opportunities Center was established in the Negro ghetto at Hunter's Point. Personnel from the schools, employment service, welfare department, and various voluntary agencies were delegated to this center to provide an integrated staff to reach the target population and to open employment opportunities in the city. Detached workers operated out of the center to establish connections with boys and girls "hanging around" on street corners.

These were all efforts to shake up the conventional institutional system a bit and move it closer to one of the crucial problems of the 1960s: unemployed, unskilled, out-of-school youth in low income, urban areas. Of course, no effort like that can be fully successful in a stagnant economy, where the jobs are not there to be had.

Work on the public account

Whenever this subject is mentioned, there is an automatic negative response among some people: "Go back to WPA? Support those loafers?" Such a response is either ill-informed or less than candid. Who is trying to kid whom? An honest look at the relationships between the government and private sectors in running the American economy will show positive government support and bolstering of private enterprise on all sides. Industry groupings in the private sector will be the first to defend this to the death, and more power to them.

The subsidies for shipping and airlines, public support of agriculture, depletion allowances in the oil industry, tariff protection across the board, and local tax forgiveness to entice new industry, clearly show that the principle of government support of the economy is an accepted part of the American way of life.

It remains to extend that support more effectively to the weaker sectors, particularly to the people who are now non-producers or marginal producers. The result over the long run will be higher production and wider and more vigorous markets.

Probably the main reason this has not yet been done with full effectiveness is that the weak do not influence legislation and executive policy. The problem is essentially the lack of political power. In the 1930s labor organized itself and increased its share of the national proceeds. At that time organized labor represented the disadvantaged and weak. This is not so true today.

One question policy-makers have to decide in the present context is: Do they want to encourage the weak and disadvantaged to organize on the basis of their weakness and deprivation against those who are strong and on top, or do they think it better to attend to the inequities and imbalances visible all around and foster measures to spread the benefits of the affluent society?

Where the economy is not using men and women who want to work, it makes sense for government to see that there is work for them. If measures to animate the economy are not fully effective in providing jobs for all who want to work, then *government should provide the jobs.* It should do so for people who have normal productive capacities as well as for those whose productive capacities are impaired because they have deteriorated, because of old age or ill health, or because their capacities never reached full power.

It is not necessary for government to "make work" to do this. There is plenty of work crying to be done. Can anyone name a public hospital, or public housing project, or jail, or mental institution, or home for the aged, or school for delinquents, or community center in any big city that could not well use additional workers at all levels of skill? Every city needs more and better public facilities: big parks, little parks, recreation areas, school buildings, libraries, day care, youth and community centers. All provide construction, maintenance, and additional service jobs. Outside of the cities there is a vast potential for productive work: national park and recreation area development, waterway development, conservation of natural resources, road and highway extension and improvement in isolated areas (e.g. the southern Appalachians and the Ozarks), schools, libraries, and other public facilities.

Within the cities there are additional services to be performed within the existing agency and institutional framework.

What does all this have to do with the slums? Some of these buildings and services are in and for the slums. Many of the jobs that would be created by these activities could be performed by people presently unemployed, and by unskilled people who are weak competitors in the open labor market (youth, the elderly, the handicapped, the ill-trained). These people live in the slums.

With the continuing advance of mechanization and automation and the concomitant rise in the level of skills necessary to fit into production processes, it is clear that for some years to come the slums will harbor substantial numbers of unemployed and underemployed. Slum conditions will not improve so long as this is the case.

Sources of accessible and inexpensive credit for low income people

One thing that victimizes poor people is seductive and usurious credit. This may be in the form of short-term, high-cost loans or installment purchase contracts with excessively high interest rates that are concealed from the unsophisticated purchaser. Partly the answer to this is education. Partly it is the provision of resources or the organization of resources to meet legitimate needs for credit at reasonable cost. This could be done through the credit-union technique or the pooling of the resources of the people of a neighborhood.

Aggressive and imaginative job development by the public employment agency

One responsibility of the employment service is "job development." This means everything from getting on the telephone and locating available jobs, to advertising in the newspapers, talking with trade and industry groups, and visiting employers. This work of the public employment service needs to be expanded and made more effective, in the light of existing and emerging conditions.

In many places concerned about unemployment, and particularly about unemployment among youth, new and vigorous efforts by the employment service to turn up jobs have usually produced more than had been expected. There are many inefficiencies in the workings of the labor market. Simply tightening the operations somewhat and facilitating the flow of applicants to available jobs reduces, to some degree, the number of unemployed.

Considerably more can be done in terms of individual job analysis and revision of entrance requirements. This is advantageous to both employer and lower-skilled job applicants. Some jobs have separable components, with differing levels of skill requirements. Analysis of jobs and reorganization of specific tasks makes it possible for the employer to pay high-skill wage rates only for high-skill work. The lower-skill operations that have been separated out as the result of the job analysis are thus available for the lower-skill worker.

For many jobs, close examination of what skills are really required shows that the advertised minimum qualifications for applicants are often unrealistically high, thus blocking out applicants who might do a job adequately.

Another thing that keeps potentially productive workers out of jobs or out of training is standard aptitude testing. Some tests are not fair to people with poor educational experience. They thus operate to exclude from work people whose ability to take a standard test is nil, but who may be able to perform a number of real-life tasks with competence. Testing procedures must be related to the realities of what is being tested for. This is a highly technical problem, but experiments (notably in the New Haven, Connecticut, Community Progress program and at the University of Chicago) have shown that it can effectively be solved.

Public employment services do not know about many job openings. Some way needs to be developed of getting all jobs, or at least more of them, registered. This could be done by giving credit on the unemployment insurance tax for job openings registered.

Many of these things can be done locally. They do not require national or even state policy or legislation.

Reawakening of trade union interest in the poor

Trade unions in the United States, with very few exceptions, no longer are predominantly concerned with lower income people. As a participant in a recorded discussion at the Center for the Study of Democratic Institutions, in 1963, said, it is beneath the dignity of most union representatives to sign a contract with a $1.35 wage rate in it. The "respectable" unions have a tendency to look only at those who are making $3 or $4 an hour. These are not the people who live in the slums. The residents of the slums, by and large, are not in the unions.

Some thoughtful union leaders are concerned about this fact, because they see the labor movement (and that is a dubious term in the 1960s) not expanding in membership, not able to make itself heard enough in matters of public policy, too often defending narrow vested interests, and frequently indistinguishable from the establishment. It would be a healthy thing were the unions to turn their attention to lower wage workers and even to the unemployed.

Extension of coverage of
social insurance, increasing the
benefits, covering more risks

Insurance in which government helps to bear the risk is important to the poor. When income is low and what comes in goes out for the costs of daily living with little or nothing going into savings or investment, unexpected interruptions of income can destroy individual or family stability. A youngster is forced to quit school and never go back; the furniture is repossessed; a job that seemed to have a future is lost; an irreversible skid downhill may begin. When a swimmer's head is just above water, and he is a weak swimmer anyway, the slightest immersion can end it all. Contrast this with the tumble of a water skier. He is a strong swimmer (he studied long enough to be one), he has on a safety belt (personal insurance), and his friends are standing by in a boat to pick him up (willing creditors, business associates, friends who will lend money).

The main risks for the poor are unemployment and ill health. Old age is also insured against, although this insurance is somewhat different. Old age is to be expected, and what is really being insured against is economic need in old age.

In America our provisions for these risks among the poor are niggardly almost to the extent of being self-defeating. Perhaps more accurately, they are ineffective in tiding a man over a temporarily rough passage—they are a straw when a rope is needed, a boy to do a man's work. Unemployment benefits are generally inadequate to support a family and carry debts until a new job is found. Health risks are not covered at all. Old age insurance payments are miniscule.

Our fears that more generous benefits will encourage dependency and laziness have been much exaggerated. A strong case can be made for the view that our miserliness results in a waste of much of what we do put into social insurance because it is not enough to accomplish its real purpose. It is like trying to dam a stream with a handful of soft mud instead of with boulders and cement. The mud is soon swept away, the cost of it wasted, and the objective of damming the stream is unaccomplished.

Extending social insurance to more people, covering the risks of ill health (and other interruptions of income) as well as unemployment, and increasing benefit payments would be important anti-slum measures. These require action at the national level, but local initiative and support in the congress can get interest aroused.

Not many people who do not live in the slums, or whose work does not make them cognizant of what goes on there, are aware of how many slum residents receive social security payments.

In New York City a study carried out by Mobilization for Youth revealed that in a population of 107,000 on the lower East Side of Manhattan (a poor area, but not rock bottom) 41.2 per cent of the families were receiving unemployment compensation, old age insurance benefits, old age assistance, aid to dependent children, or general relief.

An additional element that might well be introduced into the social security system is "mobility insurance." This would have to be planned and administered carefully. Its idea is that many marginal people remain marginal because they do not move to where the demand for labor is. They just do not know enough about labor market conditions in other places, or they do not have the reserve financial resources to go (moving expenses, paying two rents while the breadwinner goes ahead to get established before the family comes), or it is hard to pull up roots and plant them somewhere else. This last has been true of many people in depressed areas such as the mining regions of West Virginia. Even though the region cannot support its population, and this fact is well known, many people have been unwilling to move because the area is where they "belong." This tendency is particularly strong among groups whose general educational level is low. When they do not know much about the outside world, it is terrifying to contemplate leaving what they do know, even though it does not amount to much.

This was dramatically illustrated in an Ecuadorean town of 6,000 population, when an earthquake destroyed every building in the town and killed half the people. Scientists concluded that the location would very likely be hit again by earthquake at some time and recommended that the site of the rebuilt town be moved about two miles to a safer place. The townspeople refused and rebuilt their houses where they had been, because that was where they belonged.

Under the Social Security system, workers living in areas of well-established labor surplus could be encouraged, and in well-defined cases financially assisted, to move to areas of labor shortage, or at least of more active demand.

The Area Redevelopment Administration, in its efforts to revitalize depressed areas, has recognized that in certain areas there are too many people to be absorbed in the regional economy even at a revitalized level. Some of them are helped to move to other areas.

Training and retraining of adults

"You can't teach an old dog new tricks." Like most sayings, it has some truth, but another saying, often from the same culture, carries the opposite message: "It's never too late to learn." Both fit the situation of retraining or training of adults with limited skills and educational backgrounds. It can be done, but not for everyone, and it is difficult. The most extensive experience with retraining in recent years has been with people brought up in a one-industry culture and knowing nothing else, so that when the industry declined they were left almost helpless. These were the miners of the Southern Appalachian Mountains. Another group of retrainees was made up of men and women on relief. The Cook County (Chicago) Bureau of Public Aid conducted pioneering and relatively successful experiments with retraining this group.

An illustration from the Area Redevelopment program in 1962 was Mingo County, West Virginia, where unemployment was 28 per cent among the coal miners. The Area Redevelopment Administration and the Small Business Administration supplemented local resources to establish a new woodworking plant and retrain the miners, 200 of whom then found employment in the new plant. Others under the A.R.A. program were trained for logging and trucking operations. In southern New Jersey migrant "stoop laborers" were trained as farm machinery operators. In Pennsylvania miners were retrained as machine operators. In New Mexico members of Indian tribes were trained as sawmill operators. In Michigan iron miners became welders.

Mention should be made of two high quality vocational schools, Dunwoody in Minneapolis and Williamsport in Williamsport, Pennsylvania, where it has been demonstrated that adult workers can be retrained and obtain employment, even after a protracted period of unemployment. Most of these beginning efforts have been successful. It remains to be seen how effective the approach can be on a wide scale.

The Area Redevelopment Act of 1961 and the Manpower and Development and Training Act of 1962 were both designed as relatively large-scale efforts at adult training and retraining. In the Area Redevelopment Act, of course, training is only one of a variety of devices designed to upgrade depressed areas, but it is an important one.

With unskilled and under-educated adults, the main deficiency is a foundation of basic knowledge on which to build skill development. The inability to read and write, to do simple arithmetic, and to understand simple laws of nature presents an almost insuperable obstacle to skill training. There is practically no task in the modern world that does not require at least elementary knowledge of this kind.

It is extremely difficult to teach "literacy" to adults. They do not want to admit that they are illiterate or functionally illiterate (the functionally illiterate knows a little bit, but not enough to amount to anything). It is difficult to get them into a classroom. Once in the classroom they find it hard to relax and accomplish anything in that strange environment—classrooms are for children. Reaching them in their own homes or in their natural, informal groups is also difficult. And even then, the learning process for people who abandoned learning long ago, or who never had any satisfactory experience with systematic learning, is discouragingly slow.

This does not mean that efforts to train or retrain adults are hopeless. It does mean that naïve expectations about the results should be avoided. In most cases the first focus will have to be on literacy training rather than on skill training. Skill training will probably have to be aimed at not too high a level. Chicago had good experience in producing taxi drivers by training relief clients. The training plan itself should have a job at the end of it (motivation is important in adult education and nothing motivates an unemployed person like a job; nothing demoralizes like no job). In a community with limited resources careful thought must be given to priorities—which has a more demanding claim on attention and resources, training of youth or adults? In most cases the answer would have to be youth. One would hope that this need not mean abandoning efforts to equip nonproductive adults for work.

Adequate and effective public assistance programs

Financial assistance to people in need and the concomitant supporting and rehabilitative services are inadequate in the United States. Such programs should be constructive and wealth-producing. In fact, they are hardly adequate as salvage operations or even anti-starvation measures.

The average per person monthly relief payment to a needy family under the Aid to Dependent Children program in 1962 was $31.06, ranging from $9.05 in Mississippi to $49.30 in Massachusetts. The average payment to a needy blind person was $20.21; to an aged person not receiving social security benefits, $75.37. In relation to present day costs of living, these are hardly civilized standards.

The 1962 Public Welfare Amendments, characterized by President Kennedy as "the most far-reaching revision of our public welfare program since it was enacted in 1935," made some important improvements in public welfare system, but are far from sufficient. They had four major emphases.

1. A strong focus on rehabilitation and the reduction of dependency by offering states financial inducement to provide more services and training to assistance recipients.

2. Improvement of and more money for child welfare services.

3. Provision of funds for day care of children of parents who are working or seeking work and permission to assistance recipients to keep a certain amount of outside earnings without a consequent reduction of the relief payment. (E.g., an old-age assistance client may earn up to $50 per month and have only $20 deducted from the assistance).

4. Extension of assistance grants to provide federal sharing of payments to needy children where a parent was unemployed (in contrast to being absent from the home or disabled). Payments to the family (instead of only to the children and one parent). Greater federal participation in assistance to the aged, blind, and disabled in order to encourage states to increase these grants.

These improvements are still far below the level of investment which can be expected to produce new or renewed human "wealth." It is unfortunate that America has been unable to view its welfare programs as investments in human development, rather than as charity. Charity perhaps is an exaggeration, but is not too far off the mark as a description of the attitude of most local, state, and national legislators and of the general public. Welfare programs need to be regarded as investments in the growth and strengthening of people who are for one reason or another too weak to compete independently in the economy. Some recipients of assistance never will be able to compete—the totally disabled, the aged—and nothing more than decent maintenance can be offered them. But much of the human material on relief is only damaged or undeveloped. It makes economic and human sense to make a real try at capitalizing this material so that it becomes productive. The limitations on this should be only those of our technical or engineering capacity to develop or rehabilitate humans. These limitations are real enough. We should not be further limited by financial niggardliness.

More effective training for occupations

A current whipping boy in the United States is the vocational training system. Many would argue that there is no system. The harshest critics say there is only a series of schools that give limited training for skills that are usually out of date by the time the student looks for a job. This is too extreme a charge but is indicative of the fact that vocational training is ailing. This subject is relevant to the slums because most slum youth do not go on to higher education, and it is important that they be as well prepared as possible to get and keep a steady job with a future.

Just what needs to be done is still open to considerable argument, since this is a complex problem. Should the high school attempt to turn out a worker fully skilled at a particular occupation, or should it rather provide the student with a good basic general education, including, for the non-college bound, enough knowledge about electricity, machinery, and so on to prepare him for specific skill training by industry on the job or in an apprenticeship?

There is no answer to this question that will cover all situations, but the problem should be looked at nationally, as well as locally. Certainly the present articulation between high school level vocational training, post high school technical training, and industry training leaves much to be desired.

A pattern by which local communities can improve training for occupations might be the following:

1. *Industrial arts.* Industrial arts would be compulsory for all male students in the eighth and ninth grades to give them an appreciation of manual skills. The program would enable students to explore a range of skills and to better understand industry in our society. It would be purely exploratory and not for the purpose of preparing students for specific employment.

2. *Vocational guidance.* Vocational guidance would be exploratory and explanatory for both students and parents. Vocational guidance would supplement general guidance. Guidance programs would be formulated to give students a useful knowledge of industry and to encourage students who are vocationally talented or who cannot go to college to take the vocational study courses that will best develop their talents. Courses start in the eighth or ninth grade and would include simple lectures to give the students a better appreciation of the world of work and what they can best do to prepare for it. They would explain where job opportunities are, the education and training required for employment in various occupations, where

to go for a job, how to apply for a job, and so on. Guidance would continue throughout the student's school career.

3. *Employment service.* A special employment unit working in cooperation with the state employment bureau would be set up within the school to help students obtain initial employment, to organize cooperative work-study programs, and to keep in touch with students for some period of time after they have left school, whether they have graduated or not. The employment unit would identify special opportunities for employment of youth, as well as general job opportunities.

4. *Vocational courses.* Labor market studies would be made to analyze employment opportunities. The studies would be used as guides in establishing curriculums. Courses would range from practical occupational skills to pre-apprenticeship and pre-technical institute training. A pre-engineering curriculum would be introduced. Progress in skill training would be limited by progress in academic subjects only to the extent that the latter is essential to the ability of students to advance in their vocational courses.

5. *Teaching.* Academic and vocational teachers would work as a team to relate instruction in academic and vocational subjects to each other.

6. *The junior college.* A junior college would offer advanced occupational training, technician training leading to an associate degree, and a broad range of subjects leading to certificates of achievement in preparatory, retraining, and in-service programs. Instruction would be open to all persons irrespective of age and educational achievement, except as these may be essential for degrees or for specific vocational instruction.

Apprenticeship systems
must be improved

Serving an apprenticeship is a good way of getting into a trade or line of skill. For some, the apprenticeship route in the United States is an effective one. Unfortunately, the number of young men who have access to apprenticeships is far too small.

Apprenticeships are almost exclusively controlled by unions. For reasons that are perfectly understandable from the union point of view, the number of apprentices taken is often limited. This may help to keep wage rates up and maintain a fraternal atmosphere within the trade, but it is doubtful that it promotes economic growth or makes employment opportunities more available.

Apprenticeship systems have been used widely to keep Negroes out of particular trades, and this has had a direct effect in impeding improvement of slum conditions. In 1963, the crisis year in civil rights and equal opportunities, attention has been called to this situation in no uncertain terms by boycotts and picket lines. Community pressures to break down the parochial restrictions on apprenticeships can be listed in the slum improvement armory.

Another aspect of apprenticeship is that many are unreasonably long. Again, this is in response to the trade union interest in keeping the supply of labor limited so its price is high. In the general social and economic context, however, this does not help establish independent wage earners and heads of families and put more money in circulation. Efforts to shorten unreasonably long apprenticeship periods would be constructive.

A special effort should be made locally to see that youth in slum areas know about apprenticeship opportunities and that the controllers of apprenticeships give equal consideration to all. Because of past history, "equal consideration" calls for an aggressive reaching out process in slum areas to recruit applicants for apprenticeships. This act alone would do much to demonstrate to youth with low motivation that there is a chance for them.

Private employers should be
subsidized to employ
marginal workers

This suggestion has both technical and political complications. On the technical side, the question is: Which marginal workers? (Youth? The elderly? The handicapped? The low-skilled heads of families?

After this has been answered, then methods must be determined. Tax advantages could be offered or direct subsidy payments of a per cent of the wages of properly certificated marginal workers. A scrip system could be instituted, whereby the participating employer would get scrip at a reduced price. Scrip would be spent in participating stores and service establishments and redeemed by the sponsoring agency at full face value.

Although it is unlikely that the private sector will soon be able to absorb sufficient marginal low-skilled workers to maintain a healthy over-all social and economic situation, every effort should be made in this direction. Although government in one guise or another is now the largest source of employment in the United States, most employees, of course, get their pay checks from private employers. In the main, their career lines lie in the private sector. Therefore a major effort needs to be made first to encourage private employers, and then to help them, where necessary, to provide opportunities for marginal workers to work and earn a living.

Absorbing marginal workers in this way is not politically popular and goes against myths that dominate American thinking about economics and our political and social systems. Realism, however, requires that every possible course of action designed to rectify the position of the depressed parts of our population be forthrightly and objectively examined. Timely and appropriate action, such as that suggested here, must be taken before chaos forces something less desirable and valid.

It would be wise to start with younger people who are having difficulty getting good jobs. There is an urgency to develop and maintain a consistent work experience before disillusionment and disaffection become so ingrained that they shadow and distort an entire life. Wherever possible an element of skill training should be built in.

Taxes on low income families should be reduced

One of the principal features of poverty that is often overlooked is that people with low incomes don't have much money. The effects of not having much money have already been dwelt upon. Therefore, tax systems should not operate to take money away from poor people, and they often do. Sales taxes and taxes on utilities that get passed on to the consumer have this effect. The New Hampshire lottery will probably draw more money from lower income strata than higher. Effective efforts need to be made to increase the income of low income people. Policies which take away their income should be avoided.

CHAPTER V

Politics and
Citizen
Participation

THE PARTS of this heading may appear uncomfortable in such close juxtaposition. One seems unclean and the other noble and pure. Clean or unclean, they are both part of the slum picture, and not so mutually exclusive as their tone implies. They are part of the slum past, present, and future. Whether or not they offer potentials for speeding the demise of the slum is the question.

Participation in the political process

Earlier we discussed some aspects of politics: the connections between political organizations and organized crime; the political and criminal routes to respectability for some who started in the slums; the political organization as an urban adjustment service and welfare system.

"Citizen participation" is a newer term and implies the

involvement of people beyond and outside of what Robert Dahl calls the "political stratum" [1] in public affairs and community decision making. The political stratum consists of those people who take a more or less active part in politics, are well informed about local, state, and national issues, and spend a good deal of time influencing or attempting to influence public policy and action and the distribution of rewards.

The "apolitical stratum" does little beyond formal voting, and very often not even that. It may be apolitical for lack of educational breadth, distance from the political and governmental culture, absorption with personal matters, or as a reflection of a general pattern of exclusion from community life.

People who are low on the scales of social and economic status do not participate in voting as much as people who are higher. Warren Miller says that among the most disadvantaged —those with no more than a high school education, the one out of four whose family has a total annual income of less than $3,000, the southern Negro, or the unskilled laborer— voting is at best an occasional activity.[2]

In the presidential election of 1956, 54 per cent of eligible voters with incomes below $2,000, 39 per cent with incomes between $2,000 and $3,000, and 26 per cent with incomes between $3,000 and $4,000 did not vote. Only 18 per cent of those with incomes over $5,000 failed to vote. Similar rates prevailed in 1948 and 1952.

In the 1956 election, 47 per cent of the eligible voters classified as "unskilled laborers," but only 15 per cent of the "professional and managerial" types did not vote. In 1948, it was 50 per cent vs. 25 per cent, and in 1952, 40 per cent vs. 12 per cent.[3]

Probably between 60 per cent and 80 per cent of the lower

class do not belong to any formal organization. One study showed that "In every type of group, without exception— church, fraternal, recreational, patriotic, cultural—membership on the part of lower income classes was markedly lower (than the middle class)." [4]

Slum people are out

Citizen participation has relevance to improving the slum condition because one of the attributes of slum people is that they are out and they feel they are out. The world of success and the good things of life is somewhere else. Michael Harrington calls the world of the poor "the other America." The poor and the slum residents know that things are run by somebody else. They have no stake in the larger community, they do not make its decisions, and most do not expect to get anywhere in it.

The response to being out takes a number of forms: indifference to and disengagement from any affairs beyond the person or a small circle of family and friends (this is seen on all levels of American society, but in the slum it is exaggerated); alienation from the institutions and systems through which decisions are made, things are organized, human development is nourished, and the culture is perpetuated (such as the public school system); formation of subcultures with values at variance from those of the dominant culture ("If we can't play in your game, we'll have our own game with our own rules, and to hell with you"); hostility and resentment toward the "them," who push you around or don't give you a break.

Why citizen participation

The idea behind citizen participation is that it is undemocratic and un-American for large, geographically identifiable groups of people to be excluded from decision making. On a more pragmatic level, reform or improvement efforts will not get far if the people who are "improved" are not themselves engaged in the improvement process.

Some will boggle at the phrase, "people who are to be improved." This sounds arrogant and condescending. Some will say: "Here is another middle class do-gooder trying to make everybody over in his own image. Why don't they leave the lower class alone!"

This sounds good, but it just does not fit the realities of America. Earlier some of the characteristics of a lower class or slum way of life have been described. Some of these are bad, some are good, and some just are.

What we are talking about here is not an attempt to make everybody the same. Much of the dynamic of our society is lost when uniformity and homogeneity begin to ooze over the demographic landscape. But to have more money and a decent place to live, to move around freely, and not to be plagued by ill-health, bill collectors, police, and people who want to make you better requires having a steady job with an adequate wage. It requires being able to read and write, having some skill, and being reliable. Many of the people now living in the slums do not fulfill these requirements and therefore need to be improved as part of the process of improving their chances.

To repeat, then, the process of improvement is not likely

to strike very deep unless the target people themselves are part of it. In practice this means that parents must support, or at least not resist, efforts to improve slum schools and the performance of their children in those schools. The adults of a neighborhood must cooperate with and help the efforts to control delinquent behavior. They must support the pressure and political tactics designed to persuade decision makers to make the decisions that will tend to improve slum conditions.

There are various approaches to mobilizing the attention and energies of slum residents. No single approach is the right one for every situation. That such efforts can be successful has been demonstrated. That it is difficult and the outcome not always predictable has also been demonstrated. But it is a mistake to think that everyone in the slums is hopelessly beaten, defeated, at war with society, or incompetent, and that therefore they cannot do anything for themselves. If given a genuine chance, even some of the apparently defeated ones, or the ones at war, may make surprising contributions to constructive common endeavor on behalf of the community, the neighborhood, or some special group.

Phoniness not wanted

One cardinal rule about effort to encourage citizen participation is that it not be phony. People who have been pushed around, fooled, and taken advantage of for so long are inclined to think that any approaches to them from the outside world are phony. A genuine attempt to elicit citizen participation in decision making processes must be prepared to accept the fact that the participants will want to have a real voice. Sometimes the sound of the voice and the results of the expression will not be what the original sponsors of citizen participation want, because there are conflicts of interest involved and deep differences of opinion are bound to occur.

Felt needs

An organization or group of people interested in community development or a local government agency may, with all good will, wish to involve residents of a slum area in resolving some problem or in accomplishing some specific objective. This might be establishment of a day-care center, or contributing ideas to the planning of an urban renewal area, or launching a summer program for the youngsters. It may be discovered that the residents, once engaged, really want to talk and do something about *de facto* segregation in the schools, or police brutality, or unequal employment opportunities. They may want to send a delegation to city hall or make a public statement against the very agency that has helped them organize.

In community development parlance this is known as "felt needs." The question for the sponsors, or organizers, or catalyzers, is whether to allow things to go in this direction, or to cancel the project. The sponsors may not be able to cancel, but on the other hand, if the new citizen participants are not allowed to set some of the agenda themselves, they will soon lose interest.

Reference to the possibility that slum residents may get so active that they "get out of hand" or go off on what somebody else may consider a tangent may sound utopian to those who have had experience in trying to organize low income people for some kind of community or political participation. The results are very often disappointing or short-lived.

Reasons for nonparticipation

There are four main reasons why adults in low income areas do not get closely involved with community affairs. The first is residential mobility. People in the slums move from one place to another frequently. They may not move very far away, but the shifting about occurs quite often. Urban renewal contributes to this process, as does public housing. There is movement into the area, within it, and out. The last is usually a response to improved economic status.

The second reason is that most efforts to organize the community or to stimulate greater citizen participation are staffed or promoted by middle class people. To the extent that lower class people feel they are being dominated or used, they are likely to remain distant or withdraw.

Self-defeating attitudes is a third barrier to citizen participation by slum residents. Lower income groups tend to view life pessimistically and thus to resign from struggle. This defeatism, resulting in lack of participation, produces a loss of interest in changing their condition.

The fourth factor mitigating aganst citizen partcipation in the slums is intergroup tension. Where there is so much to be hostile about in the objective circumstances of life, differences along racial and ethnic lines, new vs. old, and poorer vs. not-so-poor are exacerbated and make common concern and effort even more difficult.[5]

Probably the self-defeating attitude is as strong as any of these reasons. This is another way of saying that there is a pervasive feeling of helplessness. Things are so big and far away and the people who control them unreachable. "What's the use—go fight city hall."

There is also the fact that in America, unlike Africa or Asia, the poor are in the minority, and the culture says that all you need to get ahead is individual initiative and hard work. These two facts combined make it easy for anyone who is poor to convince himself that he really is no good and that this is why he is poor. He may not say this out loud, but it is all too often present in his guts. In Warren Haggstrom's wry words: "This orientation interferes with the arduous pursuit of distant jointly held goals." [6]

Lloyd Ohlin said residents of deprived urban areas

> frequently experience an intense feeling of social isolation and alienation and lack of power, knowledge or skill to alter their condition. Mass migration, high mobility, and physical re-development of local facilities have produced a situation where structures for integrating the migrants into the larger community are either absent, damaged, or unobservable to the migrant. Under such conditions, the interests of the newcomers remain unarticulated and unmet.[7]

Many observers have said this. But when they talk about what to do about it, disagreement sets in.

The most extreme prescription, of course, is the communist one of revolution. This position argues that the established powers of the community are never going to be persuaded or negotiated into sharing their power or the good things of life over which they have control. Therefore, they have to be taken by force, and power lodged in the hands of the have-nots, the proletariat.

The use of conflict in organization

Another approach that uses conflict and political force but without destroying the established system is promoted by the Industrial Areas Foundation and its director, Saul Alinsky. Its rationale is that the holders of power are not going to relinquish or share that power, or even to allow existing institutions to follow policies and carry out actions that will improve the conditions of the poor, unless they are forced to do so by hard-nosed bargaining techniques. In order to bargain effectively, both parties must have a foundation of power upon which to stand. No bargaining takes place where the negotiators are unequal in power. Only imposed resolutions can come out of unequal power positions. In order for poor people to establish a power base, they must act in concert. To accomplish this getting together of people who live in an atmosphere of discouragement and helplessness, issues and dormant conflicts must be highlighted and exacerbated, so that the dispirited will have something to rally around and get excited about. Enemies must be identified and singled out for attack. This provides clear-cut and rousing objectives as organizational cement. Then, with this base, all the appropriate weapons in the arsenal of collective bargaining and political pressure are brought to bear— voter registration, picketing, boycotting, publicity, public meetings, threats, and so on.

This method has been clearly described by Alinsky:

In the development of an organization for democratic citizen participation . . . resentments and dormant hostilities must be brought up to visible surface where they can be transformed into problems. . . . A people do not break through their previous fatalism of submerged resentment and frustration into open problems which can be faced and dealt with until they have a mechanism, or a formula for effectively coping with these problems. . . . There can be no darker or more devastating tragedy than the death of a man's faith in himself, in his power to direct his future.[8]

A question about the deliberate use of conflict and the exacerbation of raw issues that is carried out by the Industrial Areas Foundation is how the energy thus generated gets translated into institutional change. If the response of the establishment is to be more than a gesture to placate the angry crowd or to "cool out" the potential negative votes among a group of voters, the city institutions have to change their way of doing things. The schools have to do things differently, and their hearts have to be in it if the change is to be profound. The same goes for the urban renewal agency, the buildings inspection department, the recreation department, the employment service, and so on. Many of these changes are technical in nature. They have to consist of more than generalities. Once the board of education admits that there is *de facto* segregation and that this is deleterious to education, what then? The resolution of this problem, which means education for Negro children and poor children of all races, as good as that available to middle-class white children, must to a great extent be worked out by the institution itself and its professional staff. Precisely how should the school district lines be redrawn to promote integration? What about a school deep in the center of a Negro residential area with no white residents nearby? How is reading taught more effectively to culturally deprived children? How can team teaching be used to make teaching in

slum schools more effective? These and many others are questions for which only the professional can provide the detailed
answers. The citizens' group can certainly identify and promote
broad policies, but to what extent can they get involved in
the technical details to be sure that the broad policies are
truly expressed in practice, or even that the policy is not being
sabotaged by the bureaucracy? Having attacked the established
institutions as part of the strategy of building up power, how
are the institutions and their personnel persuaded whole-
heartedly to execute the new policies and to apply their latent
creativity and imagination to develop new and different techniques, without which the general policy remains an empty
statement of good intentions? In short, how does one balance
the carrot and the stick to get the donkey going in the right
direction?

The answer is not clear. These comments are not intended
to cast doubt on the validity of militancy. Where there is injustice and inequality, militancy is to be desired and expected.
It is a legitimate part of a democratic society and is recognized as such in our constitution. The only question that is
being raised here is how militant energy and pressure gets
translated into institutional change in a society that is ever
more bureaucratically organized in both public and private sectors. The suggestion is offered here that militancy must be
accompanied by subtly getting the bureaucracy on the side of
change so they need not be exclusively identified as "the
enemy."

Cooperating with the establishment

The third kind of approach, within which there are many variations, calls for existing institutions to mobilize people and resources from all levels of the community to work jointly toward the solution of slum problems. Such efforts attempt to involve the residents of a slum area in common effort. This is done through organizations such as churches, fraternal groups, village clubs, social clubs—all the organizations which already command people's loyalty. Among a population of over 100,000 on the lower East Side of New York City, with a predominantly white population but a growing intermixture of Negroes and Puerto Ricans, over 200 such organizations were identified.

Mobilization may be accomplished through new organizations established for specific, short-range purposes, or new organizations established on a permanent basis with very general purposes, the specifics to be developed by the membership in response to the objective situation and the desires of the members.

How to judge success

Warren Haggstrom suggests that there are four criteria by which to judge whether or not local action involving the affected persons themselves is likely to be successful:

1. The person involved sees himself as a source of action; the action expresses his worth.
2. The action demands much in effort and in skill or in other ways becomes salient to major areas of his personality.

3. The action ends in success and thus enhances his conception of his own worth.

4. The successful self-originated important action increases the force and number of symbolic or nonsymbolic communications to him that he is a worthwhile person.[9]

These are valid criteria against which to assess the impact of citizen participation upon people who are not likely to have participated before.

There are other criteria, such as: What did the group get done? Did it have staying power? Did it have to be nursed along interminably? Was it taken over by a few people whose main objective was inflating their own importance? Was it able to influence large and powerful institutions? Was it able to spark desirable changes in institutional and bureaucratic methods? Who were the people really involved? Were they a true cross-section of the neighborhood or area, or were they semi-professional at the business of community organization? Was the leadership limited to people who were already on their way up and out of the slum, or did some of the leadership gravitate to people who would probably be in the slum for a longer period of time? Did the organization become "them" or did it retain the character of "us"? Studies of members of highly organized and professionalized trade unions have shown that many members think of the modern union as "them" and not "us."

The absence of trade unions in this whole question of organization of less advantaged people is an interesting and significant phenomenon. It is another indication of the general irrelevance of unions to the slum problem. Increasingly the unions have come to represent the elite of the working class and to become more and more distant from the problems and needs of the people in the lower reaches of the labor market or out of it altogether. It may be that trade unions have lost strength in part because of this. Some responsible union leadership is now urging that unions do more about low wage workers and even the unemployed. It is an open question as to whether or not the present union "establishment" could by its very nature in the 1960s effectively sponsor such a reorientation.

Sponsorship

Sponsorship of an indigenous organization or an organization that seeks real involvement of low income people presents many knotty issues. Lloyd Ohlin summarizes the main issues in this way:

> The problem of sponsorship is difficult because indigenous social movements frequently produce effects which reorder or challenge the existing structure of power in the area of activity or decision that is the target of action. To what extent can existing power structures in different areas of community activity be expected to stimulate or foster the articulation and expression of the interests of unorganized groups? . . . . The question of sponsorship raises the problem of vested interests in its most acute form. . . . Whenever existing organizations are used to sponsor indigenous social movements the primary interests of the sponsoring organization tend to affect the selection of members, the form of the organization, the specification of objectives, and determination and control of the implementing activities.[10]

One conclusion is that the sponsor must play an over-all game and not be limited to narrow objectives or particular organizations. Otherwise he becomes suspect or imprisoned.

Saul Alinsky, from a different perspective, agrees with this general principle but in more restrictive form.

> In order to be part of all, you may be part of none. In dealing with the innumerable rivalries, fears, jealousies, and suspicions within a community, the organizer will discover that not only must his own moral standing and behavior be impeccable, but that he cannot enjoy the confidence even to a limited degree of all other groups as long as he is personally identified with one or two of the community agencies.[11]

Pilot jobs

Richard and Hephzibah Hauser, working in London on the activation of less advantaged people toward achieving a "fraternal society" in contrast to what they describe as the present "paternal society" (East and West) describe the process thus:

> We think it best to proceed by means of *pilot* jobs. First, we find or form a group of people (they need not be "talented" or prominent, indeed we often work with ex-prisoners, ex-mental patients, or bottom stream secondary school children); then, by means of a survey we draw their attention to some existing social evil or injustice (better still, they spot it for themselves, once discussion and argument with us have removed the scales of paternalism from their eyes); the sight of it rouses them to indignation; next, we encourage them to turn this indignation to positive practical account by devising a way of remedying the ill (the way must be their own, since we wish to avoid all resemblance to fathers who give orders to unthinking and obsequious sons); finally the remedy is tried out, but on a small scale only. This is what we mean by a *pilot job*. By means of it we can either a) demonstrate such an easy way

of remedying the ill that the establishment has to follow our lead, or b) at least state from our experience what obstacles are to be overcome.[12]

The point of all this is that the involvement and participation of people, in this case the people of the slums, in the resolution of their own problems is a *sine qua non* if the problems are to be resolved. Solutions cannot be imposed from the outside. People cannot be made to change just by being told to do so or even told how to do so. They themselves must be engaged in the process of change. A change agent (called organizer, community developer, urban extension agent, social worker, agitator, facilitator, minister, or missionary) is important to the process to help stir things up, to catalyze, to suggest, to inform. But the ultimate motor power must come from the affected people.

Local action alone is not enough

This is not to say that all problems of the slums can be resolved by local indigenous action. They cannot. As has been pointed out before, there are broad and pervasive economic and social forces at work producing slums and slum people and many of these can only be influenced at city, state, national, and even international levels. But in the slum area itself one of the powerful contributors to a change in atmosphere and outlook and performance will be the people themselves through organization in which they have a real part.

There is a right approach

For low income people approaches and organizing and acting methods must be used that differ from those of the usual P.T.A., League of Women Voters, middle class social club, or civic association. These will be techniques that keep in mind the way people in low income areas tend to think, feel, and behave.

Frank Riessman gives some clues about this in his listing of the ways of thinking and working of people in a low income culture:

Physical and visual rather than aural. (How long can you listen to a long speech, or the secretary's report of the last meeting?)

Content-centered rather than form-centered. (Who cares how many and what kind of officers we have or what the by-laws should say? Let's get down to business.)

Externally-oriented rather than introspective. (Joe Blow got fired because the foreman didn't like him, not because he was late for work three days in a row.)

Problem-centered rather than abstract-centered. (I don't care if it's better to have a racial mix in a housing project. If Negroes need more places to live, build more housing. I don't care where it's located.)

Inductive rather than deductive.

Spatial rather than temporal.

Slow, careful, patient, persevering in areas of importance rather than quick, clever, facile.

Games and action preferred to tests.

Expressive rather than instrumental orientation.

One-track thinking and unorthodox learning rather than other-directed flexibility.

Words learned in relation to action rather than for their own sake. (Inventive word power and "hip" language.)

Translated into organization terms this means informal meetings, although not uncontrolled; not too much concentration on formal organizational matters and rules of procedure; fun at the meetings; small groups meeting at odd places like the back of the cafe or bar, as well as larger sessions in regular meeting places. Don't be afraid of conflict—it is inherent in many situations. Don't waste time on trivialities—get right to the business at hand. Keep the speeches short. Don't discourage passion as long as it does not get out of hand—passionate issues are involved, after all. Deal with specifics and name names. Don't let things get too complicated—develop a single issue to resolution or plan of action before moving on to the next or introducing side issues. Don't be high and mighty. Don't pretend to be what you are not. Be sure that no individual or group thinks he or it is being unfairly treated. Use visual aids, blackboard, and charts. Above all, be relevant —deal with the central issues.

How long does the organizer stay?

Another question outside organizers or catalyzers must face in attempting to activate and involve slum residents is how long they should stay in the picture. If the professional community organizer stays too long in a leadership or helping role, no matter how subtly acted out, he can never shed his true character as an outsider. Thus he runs the risk of weakening the local group by relieving it of the final responsibility for standing on its own feet.

Most experienced organizers would agree that they must withdraw after the initial period of organization. This is consciously done by the Hausers in London and by Alinsky and is recommended by Ohlin.

The need for an outside catalytic agent is denied by no one. Nicholas von Hoffman, Supervisor of the Woodlawn Project for the Industrial Areas Foundation, had this to say on that subject:

> New forms and patterns of action have often come about only when an outside element has been added to the political chemistry. Many revolutions, be they violent or non-violent, are traceable to outsiders. Moses, whatever his blood pedigree, grew up an Egyptian. Lenin was a worker no more than Clement Atlee, and the Frenchmen who were the school masters of the American revolution were certainly not provincial colonists. The outsider is often the final and indispensable catalyst for change. Outsiders are customarily less likely to fail to see the forest for the trees. Their fresh viewpoint opens men's eyes to new formations, new tactics, to the road that goes toward the constitution of a new order.[13]

The political system

It is clear from the foregoing discussion that if citizens are going to participate and get involved in local activities to accomplish specific ends, they must also be involved with the conventional political system. Many decisions made by government concerning local needs, as put forward by the organized residents of a slum area, will be influenced by people whose primary commitment is to the regular partisan political system.

There is often an unfortunate separation between citizen participation and politics for people concerned with this subject. The two should be intimately linked. After all, the political system is supposed to serve the needs of the people. It will only serve those needs effectively if people use it and demand that it perform. If people consider politics beneath their dignity, or so closely controlled by "them" that it is not worth the attempt for the broader good, they will leave a vacuum and invite those who would use it for narrow ends, personal aggrandizement, or chicanery.

Citizen participation is essentially a political process serving political ends in the broadest sense of the term. Efforts to involve local residents in common action therefore should unabashedly demand that the aldermen, the councilmen, the political committeemen, and other elected officials support the moves designed to improve the conditions of the slums and near-slums.

Referring less euphemistically to one aspect of citizen participation, Carl Feiss, writing in *Architectural Forum* (April, 1962), stated what he considered the central point: "The basic weakness of slum programs since the earliest days is that slum people have not been storming city hall to get out of the slums." [14]

S. M. Miller has some strong words on this subject:

> Many social actionists articulate the position that they try to keep their social action programs uncontaminated by partisan political maneuvering. As with other positions I have criticised, there is obvious merit in this outlook. But again it has its drawbacks. Let's face it—no community of the poor can solve all its problems by itself even if it is very effectively organized and can make City Hall grease its squeaks before

any other. National, federal action is going to be needed to handle the production and maintenance of poverty. The poor have to be an effective political force within the political parties to get far reaching results. Poverty, e.g., unemployment, cannot be fully handled on a neighborhood by neighborhood basis.

If the poor were effectively organized and if they really turned out at the polls and if their vote were deliverable (i.e. class and ethnic issues really determined their voting rather than candidate personality and the like), then they could be a political force at both city and national levels and could get things done which really cut into their problems.

But many social actionists are political purists and do not want involvement in politics. But if social action is successful where is it to go—but to political parties? [15]

On the same subject, Nicholas von Hoffman writes:

. . . the whole discussion (is) in the domain of politics. The arrangement of society and the conduct of the state are more than anything else, the proper business of politics. Community and politics, as the words are usually used, are things apart— but are they?

He answers "No," and quotes Aristotle, Montesquieu, and Ortega y Gasset to support the point.[16]

Some citizen participation experiences have been faced with the dilemma of the natural tendency to use organizations as routes to political office. The citizens' organization is a place where a man can become known, his leadership qualities established, and a record made. It is not surprising, nor is it undesirable, that some people should see the pursuit of public office as a natural sequence. What has to be guarded against here is the misuse of the organization for partisan purposes by the candidate. As soon as he becomes an avowed candidate, he must withdraw from official leadership in the citizen organization.

In one city, the Urban Redevelopment Agency undertook to stimulate the organization of block clubs and neighborhood associations to support and to contribute to urban renewal planning. Skeptical observers thought they saw in this a somewhat cynical attempt to build up a new quasi-political organization to support urban renewal, because neither of the two conventional political parties was very enthusiastic about it. Such an effort is open to question because the real purpose will not long be secret, and disillusionment and hostility are likely to replace enthusiasm. Seeking citizen participation in urban renewal planning and seeking citizen support for an established urban renewal plan are two different animals. Noble as the motives of the urban renewers might have been, this effort to stimulate citizen involvement was phony and thus violated rule number one.

Middle class and lower class relationships

Another question organizers of the indigenous will have to face is whether or not working class people and middle income people can function together in one organization. It is doubtful that they can.

There are some middle class people who are concerned about the deplorable conditions in the slums and want to remedy them. Or there are middle class people who live close enough to slum areas or areas on the way to being slums, or in enclaves surrounded by slums to be included in the local organization. The trouble is that the middle class people are representative of what the low income people have not got, and as a group represent the enemy or "them." It is hard to talk and think freely with people who go home to a different world. In addition, the middle class people tend to be able to speak better, to be more familiar with what to do in a meeting, to know more about the theory or general context represented by any particular problem, and to know their way around the institutions and agencies of the city. In short, they represent stiff competition in organizational maneuverings and they are likely to take over or to be handed leadership and to nurture diffidence or hostility among the less educated, low-income members.

Herbert Gans made some observations about this in connection with a specific local experience in Chicago, the Hyde Park-Kenwood Community Conference.

Pretty much like all such groups, the Conference, moving along by organizational and social skills alien to working- or lower-class people, was unable to enroll the non-middle class population in its system of block organizations. The plain fact is that, despite the rhetorical claims of citizens' groups to be even more widely representative than any political party, their actions suggest they respond above all to the special interests of their dominant middle class membership. This eventually happened in the Hyde Park-Kenwood renewal. When the Conference was asked to support the University of Chicago's plan, it had in effect to sanction the latter's relocation of large numbers of poor Negroes—a matter contrary to the group's declared racial convictions. . . . Unable in the earlier years to enlist the participation of poorer residents, the Conference branded them as apathetic; but when, on the plan's being made public, some of these "apathetic" elements rose up in a militant protest movement, the Conference then rejected the action, refusing to call it "citizen participation." [17]

The early onset of class divisions is sensitively described in a letter from Mrs. Deborah Meier, a substitute teacher in Chicago, to her mother, Mrs. Joseph Willen, President of the National Council of Jewish Women. The letter, written in February, 1964, states:

> I taught an eighth-grade class this week. . . . The class, a departmental set-up in which I was the English teacher, went well. Of the four groups, including the homeroom, only one was unruly and chaotic.
>
> But with children this age, one is depressingly impressed with the strength of their resistance to learning. The middle class kids try out their tricks on you, but they obviously hope you will "win" and get a chance to teach them.
>
> The others have deep seated resistance to the learning process—it involves them in a relationship to life from which they have long since blocked themselves off. Hope, expectations, "illusions" are too painful . . . to engage in, and in the manner so common to the neurotic, they have many defenses against such pain. Mostly the defense of apathy and cynicism. They have their "fun" and games, and are even quite likeable, as long as you do not try to "get through." It would require for most of them a real emotional-intellectual crisis—and supportive help to sustain it—for them to make the leap into the realm of academic values.
>
> A really good teacher, I suppose, can play a part in producing or supporting such a crisis for a few children. I suppose a regular teacher must get her pleasure out of the feeling that she has produced a small spark that may lead to or encourage such a crisis, or that in rare cases she has been the final spark setting such a crisis off and can help sustain it long enough to produce some achievements, some victories and some

pleasures that can begin to offer themselves as replacements for the concomitant pain which ambition will cause them.

But with a class of 30-35 kids, in a system designed to produce the opposite, how rare must be those moments when a teacher can "get through."

I suppose that is an additional reason why smaller and younger children appeal to me, for permanent teaching. While it is partially an illusion of my own it seems as though one may be able to create this "crisis" more easily, less painfully and more permanently with a young, less hardened and less apathetic child. By 8th grade there is not only the general psychic resistance to hope, but the specific hostility to all the violence that the school system (not to mention life) itself represents.

In sum, it is probably too much to hope for that middle class people and lower class people can work effectively together over a long period of time in a citizen organization. Perhaps this is too pessimistic. Evidence to the contrary would be refreshing. But so far there is little evidence or logic to support the opposite view. This does not mean it should not be tried. It does not mean that it cannot work for short-run, specific purposes where lower class and middle class interests are clearly parallel. It does not mean that a community should not aggressively pursue a policy of appointing blue collar representatives to official public and private boards, committees, and councils. And it does not mean that officialdom and the holders of power in the private sector should not encourage organization of low income people and listen seriously when they have something to say. All of these things most certainly should be done. It is only to say that no one should be too optimistic about the lambs and the lions.

One writer who has contributed much to our knowledge

about social classes in America, W. Lloyd Warner, has expressed his concern about this in these terms: "If we cannot eliminate a system of class status, we can and must work to keep it as democratic as possible. To be successful we must see to it that each American is given his chance to move in the social scale. This ideal of equality of opportunity is essential for our democracy." [18]

Participation as status raiser

Participation in community affairs and decision making is one of the routes to upward mobility. Witness the policy of many companies to encourage their employees to play a part in community activities and voluntary organizations, and the readiness of "busy" businessmen to accept appointment to boards and committees of respectable organizations seeking to improve the community. Social status is partly derived from and enhanced by these activities. Why not consciously apply this principle to the task of raising the status of low status people? Such an effort will accomplish a number of ends. It will raise the status of the leaders of lower groups; it will demonstrate to the low income community that the larger community is interested in hearing their point of view; it will provide "success models" for people in the slum to show that some of them can go up; and last, but far from least, it will introduce some new perspectives, insights, understandings, ideas, and realism into the community deliberations about some of its social and economic problems.

The mechanics of such an operation are fairly easy. The ingredients that are in American communities today are interest, appreciation of what it can accomplish, and determination by community leaders to press reluctant organizations to cooperate.

A simple survey of boards and committees in the community will show how few blue collar and minority group representatives participate in them—an activity that is assumed to be so central to the American way of life. It is central for a part of our population, but foreign to a very large segment.

Pushing this forward in a community can best be done by a small group of top influentials, without excessive fanfare. It should be done organization by organization or committee by committee, each being approached according to its particular circumstances. This should be accompanied by two other actions simultaneously: the development of a list of or information about potential leaders from low income areas, and a quiet, informal briefing operation with the cooperating boards and committees on aspects of working with representatives of unfamiliar low income groups.

Where something of this sort has been tried, two complications have tended to arise. People say: "We are willing to get someone but we can't find a really qualified person." This may sometimes be true, but the chances are that resources have not been tapped in a thorough and sophisticated way. There are likely to be many unrecognized leaders in the low income community. Second, the wrong kind of leader, or a leader who does not have followers, or whose leadership is out of date, may be selected. This is particularly true among Negroes. It has long been customary for the white community to call on a selected list of Negro "leaders." The experience of "the same old faces" showing up is common everywhere. The trouble is that some of these traditional leaders are not in tune with the fast-moving recent developments in the Negro community. They may be responsible and unpolitical and not emotional, but they do not really represent the predominant feelings and attitudes among Negroes today. They may even be "Uncle Toms" in the eyes of the majority of Negroes. If this is the case, they cannot perform their expected function in the larger community. It is better to seek out people who are an integral part of the new dynamism among Negroes since they represent the real strengths upon which to build.

Decentralization of local government

Another interpretation of what citizen participation might mean is decentralization of governmental authority and functioning. This is a complicated area and one which needs some fresh thinking and experimentation. One city has even talked about setting up something like district city halls, strategically located around town, particularly in the densely-populated areas including the slums.

It is equally difficult to generalize about this theme and to lay down precise patterns that can be recommended with confidence. But some things can be said about the idea. These comments are limited to the subject of citizen participation and do not refer to governmental efficiency and effectiveness.

Obviously, many of the functions of city government can only be carried out centrally, or if they are districted, there is no room for citizen participation in them. This would be true of tax assessment and collection, for example.

It might seem also to be true of police and fire protection, but on second thought it is clear that this is not so. In both police and fire protection there may well be room for local citizen participation on an area or district basis. A citizens' advisory group for a precinct might help bring police and citizen closer together. Because people from the area are identified with it, it could interpret the attitudes of the citizenry (who may be hostile toward the police), support the efforts of the police, and exercise a general pressure in the community toward respect for the law and its representatives. Fire prevention requires cooperation of the residents of the district. This cooperation is likely to be more meaningful if residents of the area are invited to join with the professional firemen to plan and help carry out fire prevention activities in the district.

Many more illustrations could be uncovered by a little thought about each function of local (and even higher) government. That thought process itself is something that representatives of city hall could invite the local residents to participate in. They could think through ways in which citizens can aid local government and bring government closer to the people it is serving.

There may even be possibilities in connection with the courts. There is some serious thought now in the United States about the desirability and feasibility of decentralized lay panels making some decisions in juvenile court cases. Some members of these panels would be residents of slum areas. Something akin to this system is in existence in England and the Scandinavian countries. There obviously must be legal safeguards, and probably each panel should have a lawyer on it. But, however the details might be worked out, there may well be a role for lay participation in this judicial process which affects the lives of so many low income families. In many slum areas, as high as 75 per cent of the children and youth are in the hands of the police and courts before they are out of their teens.

An example

One approach to organizing the unaffiliated is worth describing in broad outline since it represents a recent experience and was planned after a careful canvassing of related experiences over the country. It is part of the Mobilization for Youth program on the lower East Side of New York City. The program's primary focus is the prevention and control of juvenile delinquency, but it approaches this objective on a very broad community basis, recognizing that juvenile delinquency is a reflection of the social and economic context in which it takes place.

The rationale of the citizen-participation aspect of the program is given as follows:

> What we have said thus far suggests that we must increase the willingness and ability of local residents to participate in the social and political life of their community. Participation by adults in decision making about matters that affect their interests increases their sense of identification with the community and the larger social order. People who identify with their neighborhood and share common values are more likely to try to control juvenile misbehavior. A well-integrated community can provide learning experiences for adults which enable them to serve as more adequate models and interpreters of community life for the young. In short, there is an inverse correlation between community integration and a low rate of juvenile delinquency.[19]

The "Starter Program" of Mobilization for Youth was designed to accomplish the following objectives: to initiate contact and communication between local residents of influence and Mobilization staff members; to increase local leaders' knowledge of and interest in community affairs without diminishing their in-group influence; to stimulate leaders' motivation to take action on social issues; to develop leaders' skills in social action; to recruit paid, part-time community organizers; to increase professional knowledge of lower class styles and the potentiality of community action.

The program assumed that it would be easier to engage persons already involved in some form of group life than to reach persons who were isolated or not part of any organized activity.

Leaders of the three hundred organizations in the area were identified—the formal leaders as well as the real decision-makers, who often are not the official leaders. Where the actual leadership of a group was in doubt, more than one person was invited to attend a series of ten to fifteen meetings. Varying strategies were used to induce attendance at these meetings. For example, contributions were offered to certain groups for their cooperation. Meetings were handled by personnel sympathetic toward and understanding of the local life style.

Groups consisting of ten to fifteen leaders were formed. Careful grouping was important because some groupings would be like oil and water. The leaders of store front churches, for example, which enjoin their members from smoking, dancing, and drinking, may have been loath to come together with leaders of social clubs whose activities they considered frivolous. A mixture of "naïve" and "sophisticated" leaders was sought so that the sophisticates would not overwhelm the naïves. The meetings revolved around the social and economic problems of the area, who was doing what about it, and specific plans for broad or narrow action.

After this series of getting acquainted meetings, plans for the involvement of the organizations and the leaders as individuals were developed. Some of the leaders joined the over-all program as paid indigenous organizers on a part-time basis, so they didn't lose their primary identity and become social workers.

The functions of the organizers were to encourage greater interaction and cooperation among small groups; develop more ambitious and creative social and cultural programs; document specific grievances or abuses; stimulate social action on dramatic, readily soluble issues; increase the use of social resources by individual members; and form new small groups.

A variety of linkages between the small groups and larger groupings, on geographical or interest basis, was developed according to the desires of the individual groups and their suitability for linkage.

Program content undertaken by the groups under the new stimulus varied widely, as would be expected. Some groups are more expressive, preferring socializing, athletics, dances, cultist religious worship, and the like. Others are more instrumental, engaging in activities with serious long range goals— P.T.A.s, tenant associations, or unions. Some are willing to take part only in such undertakings as a large dance or a campaign against slum landlords. Others may be willing to take on a number of issues and do all the daily dirty work necessary. Social action issues were determined by the participants.

The paid organizer in such situations saw that the abuses or injustices being complained about were documented and not just based on rumor.

The organizer also helped to identify and document issues such as how many building violations landlord X might be guilty of, whether post office truckers neglect to make afternoon mail pickups, whether officials "pick on" Negroes and Puerto Ricans. A preliminary survey in the area showed that four problem areas were regarded as critical by the residents: juvenile behavior, housing needs, governmental service, and discrimination.

An interesting aspect of this program is that it does not rely exclusively on altruism. The theory is that middle class people participate in social action of one kind or another as a matter of course and see the connection of their activity with the long-range goal, and their own long-range self-interest. Lower class people, on the other hand, have more difficulty in relating seemingly remote goals to their immediate bread and butter problems. The Mobilization for Youth program attempts to take account of this fact by offering such benefits to participants as free legal advice, job referrals, homemakers, and baby sitters.

As time goes on, the organizer encourages autonomy and independence of the groups while still maintaining their close ties and cooperation with the over-all program. Mobilization for Youth wishes to divest itself of sponsorship of the groups as soon as possible, in the hope that an enduring commitment to the program, to the broader community, and to community action will have been built in by the time the organizer leaves.

The program's success in getting people involved was proved in early 1964, when 23 school principals in its area demanded publicly that the director of the program be fired. In their view, he had encouraged groups of parents to disrupt the orderly conduct of school business through their new indigenous organizations. The local organizations, on the other hand, felt that the school bureaucracy was insensitive to their needs and problems and did not even respect them enough to give them adequate hearing.

Such an incident indicates that people are involved and that they are dealing with important issues. It is to be hoped that open warfare is not the only result, although it is apparent that this cannot always be avoided if real problems are to be addressed.

Beyond the local area

A final word should be given about citizen participation and local indigenous organization. Many of the solutions to the underlying slum-producing conditions lie beyond the neighborhood or district. This has been said *ad nauseam* in the preceding pages and will be said again. Its relevance at this point stems from the need for action by local organizations within the context of the total community.

This is important for two main reasons. The first is that some of the targets for action lie outside the district. These may be such things as policy on school districting and segregation, on property assessment or building code enforcement, on discrimination within labor unions. These are not matters of just getting more and better services for a particular neighborhood or district. They must be corrected on a city-wide basis and made part of policies that affect the whole city.

The second reason is that a vigorous local organization

may be effective at getting things done for its own area, but this may very well be at the expense of other areas. The squeaky wheel may get the grease, but areas just as much in need may get nothing more because they have no organization to squeak, or they may actually be further deprived in some respects in order to provide grease for the squeaky wheel. Building inspectors or health inspectors, for example, may be transferred to the organized area simply because they have been demanded and it is wise politically to respond to the demand. Such a response, however, does not mean that new inspectors have been added to the total staff. Inspectors may merely have been shifted from another area where they would not be missed or where complaint has not been effectively organized. The obvious solution is that all slum areas should be organized. However, it just is not likely to happen, and organized areas should therefore not lend themselves to a process of robbing Peter to pay Paul.

The rapid pace of the Negro revolution in America is introducing a great deal of ferment and change into the subject of citizen participation. Almost anything that is committed to paper today may be out of date tomorrow. New kinds of people are getting involved in organizing in the ghetto; new methods, new targets, new structures, new motivations are all about. Black nationalism engages people who have never been engaged before. The civil rights organizations such as NAACP and CORE pull more and more people into participation. The student movements that combine civil rights objectives with social reform and opportunities for individual service (Student Non-Violent Coordinating Committee, Students for a Democratic Society, Northern Student Movement) organize and stimulate involvement on the part of ghetto residents.

Recently, the rent strike as a technique for mobilizing people has enjoyed a comeback. This is a subject that is very immediate and very angering to slum residents. No matter how fervent the promises of the local political authorities nothing seems to happen. The rats prosper. The heat fails. Plaster falls. Roaches abound. Paint peels. The landlord often cannot be found or even identified. The rent strike calls for paying rent into a fund and not passing it along to the rent collector until and unless something is done about the legitimate complaints about the building. More often than not the complaints are about conditions that are in violation of some city ordinance.

Some people involved in rent strikes feel that strikes have proved a very effective device for mobilizing slum residents to protest their lot in a manner that gets city wide attention and sometimes some results. They have also provided a good school for leadership. Nothing teaches leadership like leading.

Others who have been as deeply involved have doubts that the rent strike is worth the tremendous amount of time and energy that goes into it. In the long run, the local government must enforce the minimum legal conditions of housing decency and it is not certain at all that the rent strike can be sustained and powerful enough to get government to accomplish this. The problem of raising and maintaining standards of housing is so complicated, that even the organization of purchasing power to exert pressure for change cannot yet be considered successful.

CHAPTER VI

The Physical Environment

People concerned about slums are of two types: one sees nothing but bad buildings, the other nothing but bad tenants. They turn the discussion into a variant of which came first, the chicken or the egg, with equally profitable results.[1]

Harry Barnes in 1931 was ahead of his time in making the statement above, but, happily, it cannot be made today. The circular and mutually-reinforcing effects of all the elements that produce and maintain slums are too well recognized for anybody with an ounce of awareness to fall into the chicken-and-egg trap.

This is not to say that some things are not more important and more relevant than others, or that there is likely to be more reward in certain types of action than in others. One of the major themes of this book is that it is a complex of interrelated and interacting forces producing and maintaining slums; that the slum problem has to be attacked from many directions and at many different levels; but that there are priorities and not all relevant actions are equally potent.

Certainly, in the United States, there was an imbalance in the attack on slums in the 1930s and in the 1950s. Hopes were too high for slum clearance and public housing in the 1930s. They were too high for physical urban renewal in the 1950s. Neither of these activities was a total loss—far from it. But they did not accomplish the objectives officially established for them, in terms of reducing the extent of the slums and the iniquity of slum life. In the slum clearance and public housing programs of these years bad buildings were demolished, decent dwelling units constructed, and thousands of poor families rehoused.

In the urban renewal programs of the 1950s, these, plus other objectives, were accomplished. Refurbishing of central business districts was begun, middle income housing in the inner city was fostered and subsidized, and new tax sources in the new housing, industrial, and commercial properties were established in a number of cities.

But these efforts, plus the outflow of parts of the city population to fringe and suburban areas, did not make a dent on the problem of slum diminution that anyone could really be proud of.

There are fewer people living in dilapidated housing units today than there were in 1950. It is not accurate to say that as fast as you clean out one slum another appears, or that no headway has been made toward improving the general housing stock. Although the data from 1960 and 1950 on this score are not exactly comparable, it is safe to say that the proportionate number of substandard dwelling units and the number of people living in them has decreased. In 1950 there was no "deteriorating" category, and some of the houses designated as dilapidated in 1950 would have been included in the deteriorating category in 1960. Even taking this into account, it is clear that progress has been made. The Housing and Home Finance Agency estimates that in 1950 approximately 20.5 million people lived in urban slums and that in 1960 the number was 12.5 million.[2] That is certainly progress, but is no reason for complacency. The number is still far too high for an affluent society.

What are some of the main lines of attack on the physical aspect of the slum, the priorities, the specific types of action, and the broad public policies that should underlie them?

The slum is just one part of the city

Another dimension of the interrelatedness of all aspects of the slum should be emphasized. Up to this point particular stress has been laid on functional interrelatedness—social, economic, physical, and cultural. It is equally important to remember that the slum is part of a total geography. Measures addressed to the physical characteristics of the slum will fail or be weakened if they are out of context with the policies and actions in the total geography of which the slum is a part. Differential code enforcement in another part of town may well have a direct effect on a slum. Zoning changes elsewhere may affect it. Redevelopment of another area may overcrowd it more. Restrictive zoning in suburban areas of the same metropolitan region will most certainly affect the chances of changing the inner city slum. Land use patterns and the location of industry are vital influences. The nature of the governments of the entire metropolitan region and the degree to which they submerge parochial interests to the general interests of the region are influences.

As this book has emphasized all along with reference to policies and actions aimed at strengthening human beings, local action alone will not be adequate to the task. All levels of government must cooperate and encourage private citizens to invest and to behave in a manner which will tend to upgrade the physical environment and to provide opportunities for the residents of its poorer sections.

The role of government

The role of government should be to adopt regulatory, lending, insuring, investing, and taxing policies that will encourage the private building of housing for lower income people in the city and outside of it, will take some of the excess profits out of overoccupied and under-maintained slum properties, and will stimulate the organization of the building industry along more modern, mass-production lines, using new materials and techniques and reducing some of the cost-increasing restrictive practices (often imposed by the building trades unions) that now characterize it.

Meyerson, Terrett, and Wheaton expressed a sound approach to the situation:

> . . . the answers rest upon five general assumptions. . . . The first is that there exist neglected opportunities for profitable enterprise in housing. The second is that the time is ripe for the industrialization of housing—that is, for its heavier capitalization, for increases in labor productivity, and for decreases in costs. The third is that the consumer will respond to im-

provements in housing by spending more of his income for it. The fourth is that the federal government can play its most effective role by fostering competition on the part of investors, by widening the range of effective choice open to consumers, and by experimenting with and testing its own policies in housing and community development. The fifth is that the impulse for change and the vitality to bring change about do exist in the mind and actions of public and private leaders of the country and of its urban communities.[3]

This is not to minimize the role that government will have to play. Any realistic appraisal will recognize, with neither naïve enthusiasm nor bitter hostility, neither sentimentally nor over-emotionally, that government will and should play a leading part in tackling the slum problem. This inescapable conclusion arises from two facts: the slums are where the poor reside and this is not the market to which private enterprise looks for legitimate profits, and the meshing and harmonizing of the huge and complex forces at work producing slums can only be accomplished by the entity that represents the broad public interest, namely, government.

The trick is to assess and develop the proper roles of public and private sectors, and to keep them both dynamic. The public good must be served through government without inhibiting private enterprise nor inequitably subsidizing one section or another of it. This has happened with some builders under past urban renewal practices, certain industries that have gotten tariff protection through political pressure, and agricultural producers under a farm policy devised for other days and other circumstances.

The federal government

Since the slum problem is a national problem (as is the "urban" problem, and the "metropolitan," and the "megalopolitan"), the federal government would diminish its leadership at the risk of chaos and decay. It not only has the responsibility for taking a strong lead in view of the nature of the problem, it also has the resources of power and money that must foster and back up action. It also has intellectual resources not available uniformly at other levels of government. This is not to say that the federals are smart and states and locals are not. The broad scope and opportunities of national government are attractive to people committed to public affairs, and in the forefront of the development of national policy and practice one is likely to find more intellectual ferment and excitement than in most state and local governments. One of the most important ingredients of an effective attack on the slum problem will be the quality of the ideas that go into it. These are the most precious elements—the inventions, and innovations, and program constructions, growing out of active brains and imaginations putting the pieces together out of analysis, creative synthesis, and practical experience. Inventions in public policy, such as the withholding income tax, mortgage insurance, and parity payments, did not flower in an atmosphere of routine bureaucracy.

Thus one of the important features of the federal role should be broad program development, either for direct execution by the federal government, subvention through other levels of government, or recommendations to state and local governments. This also implies technical assistance, whether or not accompanied by financial contributions. The two main elements of the federal role are therefore program and policy development and financing.

State government

State governments should take a much stronger hand than they have taken. The logical evolution of their role has been inhibited in part by unequal representation of urban and rural areas in state legislatures. Since the Supreme Court reapportionment decision there are possibilities of redressing the imbalance at least to some degree so that urban problems can begin to get the state's attention and resources that they deserve in the state's own direct interest. It is more correct to say that the *metropolitan areas* will acquire more power, because it is the suburbs that have the increased population rather than the inner city.

Many people have despaired of expecting constructive leadership in this field on the part of state governments. In such moments of despair they often dream of enhanced direct relationships between the federal government and local government along the lines of present urban renewal and housing programs. In extreme depression they abolish state governments altogether and substitute a regional level of government, defined on some rational pattern of resources, geography, and transportation. This is fun, but should occupy only those hours at the end of the day when the human mind needs refreshment through fantasy.

In fact, it seems likely and desirable that there will continue to be a skein of direct relationships between federal agencies and local governments and that these will increase in quantity and complexity. This is inevitable when the metropolitan complexes are daily becoming more dominant focal points of so many streams of life.

The states are not going to change their nature within a span of time for which it is reasonable to plan. It therefore behooves people who want to see things done better to include state government in their thoughts. There is little question that state governments are in a position to contribute materially to the fight against slums much more effectively and efficiently than they have heretofore.

One can start from the point that local governments exist by virtue of state law. It is in state law that their powers and responsibilities are based. It follows from this that state law can enhance the capacity of local governments to discharge their responsibilities. It can enhance their ability to take some appropriate local measures to discourage slum development and to help slums that already exist to wither away.

First, in the matter of strengthening governmental capacity, the state government can take initiative in developing special-purpose or functional bodies to deal with particular aspects of the urban problem on a regional or metropolitan basis. This might include such matters as transportation, air pollution, sewage disposal, or tax equalization. These matters obviously transcend the boundaries of any local political unit.

One might ask: Why be so modest? Why talk just about special-purpose bodies? Should not the metropolitan government take in not only the central city but also its hinterland—the suburbs and satellite towns that are an integral part of the city itself but that have been unwilling to admit it?

Metropolitan government

Nothing is the matter with metropolitan government. It would be highly desirable. Blood, sweat, and tears have gone into the struggle to get metropolitan government in a number of places in the United States, but with practically no success. Dade County (Miami), Florida, and Toronto are about the only places that have been able to come near it, and even they are far from the ideal model of metropolitan government. Kansas City and Houston have approached the matter in a somewhat different manner by annexing vast areas of contiguous territory and avoiding the question of governmental reorganization. St. Louis and Cleveland made noble attempts to change to metropolitan government. Their efforts were a crashing failure.

The complex forces against a head count choice of metropolitan government seems to be just too powerful. People who have moved to the suburbs do not want to be saddled with the problems of the city they left behind, nor to pay for them. They do not want to have their higher suburban standards lowered by mixing everything in under one government embracing city and suburb. They do not want to mix with Negroes and Puerto Ricans and lower class people.

Ultimately it is to be expected that the movement will be toward regional or metropolitan governments with comprehensive local powers. For the present, it seems more practical to think in terms of something short of that.

Special arrangements

The state government can authorize city governments to exercise initiative and flexibility in establishing organizational machinery to carry out housing and redevelopment activities and to take full advantage of available federal aid.

Some state constitutions, notably that of California, allow city, county, and state governments or combinations thereof to contract to exercise their powers jointly for particular purposes. This device should be encouraged universally. It applies not only to powers related to the physical environment, but to social programs as well. Many generalizations made in this chapter concerning the enhanced role of state government likewise apply across the board.

Constitutional limits on local taxation and debt are often unrealistic and restrict the capacity of local government to cope with its problems. These should be liberalized or abolished in order to give the local government greater freedom in deciding how and to what degree it will undertake financial liability. The state can also help localities devise effective and equitable revenue systems that harmonize with state revenue needs and balance the requirements of both. When one thinks of the frequent wars between city and state governments over these questions it may seem naïve to hope that there can be some common effort toward the development of productive and just revenue systems. It may be, but it is worth the effort to try.

State government can provide local government with useful guidance in areas other than financial, such as planning, zoning, housing policy, and other matters that require a high level of technical competence. States should not be reluctant to establish grant-in-aid programs for localities to improve the urban environment. There is ample precedent for state aid to localities; this is particularly evident in public education. Nevertheless, much progress can be made toward using grants-in-aid to encourage local governments to go after their slum problems more aggressively and in a more integrated manner than they have been doing. The case for this is strong, given the facts of the basic responsibility of the state for local government and the wider range of revenue sources normally available to the state. One thing that has retarded this kind of development is the imbalance in legislative representation of urban and rural populations.[4]

The role of government at any level *vis-à-vis* housing and the physical environment is to so arrange its intervention that the particular mode of intervention can be changed. This is easier said than done (a good many things in this book are easier said than done), but is nonetheless important. Specific laws, or regulations, or policies might be made automatically terminable so that they have to be reviewed within some reasonable period of time. When government applies its muscle to any sphere of activity, that muscle is likely to grow stronger. There is nothing objectionable about this in itself. The trouble is that with exercise, particular muscles may develop at the expense of others, and once established, this dominance is difficult to reverse.

In plain English the point is this: Policies and practices are invented by people at particular times under particular circumstances. People are not all-knowing and circumstances change. Experience may show that a major policy is wrong or inadequate in certain respects, or circumstances may change so that a major policy established five or ten years before is unsuited to the present. The determinants of the human condition are so complex that no one person or group of persons can get them all into proper perspective and give them proper weights. People are bound to be wrong about some of them and to devalue others or leave them out of consideration altogether. Likewise, the changes taking place in so many sectors are so rapid and kaleidoscopic they cannot be accurately predicted. Further, a single unforeseen event may throw all well-laid plans into a cocked hat. When the cheap and easy method of birth control is invented, changes are going to take place in many parts of the world. If atomic weapon and armaments control and reduction become dominant international policy, big economic changes will take place.

Public housing is an example of a good idea, the full effects and implications of which were not immediately seen. The emphasis on large, high-rise buildings located in low income areas of big cities should have been changed earlier. It has not completely changed yet, but the movement is definitely away from this solution for the housing needs of low income families. Many thousands of people are now housed in sound physical structures with all the necessary plumbing facilities. Many thousands of them are also trapped in ghetto-like living arrangements while the real estate of public housing is frozen for many years to come.

One further general observation follows, before a list of shoulds, cans, musts, and might be considereds. People are moving out of the inner city to fringe and suburban areas. This is a trend amply documented by the 1960 census and analyzed in depth by Raymond Vernon and his associates in their study of the New York metropolitan region.[5]

The core city is thinning out. Industry, commerce, and

residents are spreading out over the landscape. This trend is not limited to white collar workers who then commute back to the central business district. Blue collar workers are also moving out, following the industrial plants and commercial centers. Policy and practice, with reference to the city slum, need to keep this trend in mind and in perspective. People breathe a sigh of relief and say: "Well, if we just sit still long enough, the current demographic trends will dry up the slums and we do not have to take positive action to speed the process. Let us turn our attention to the evolving problems of the fringe and suburban areas." This is an oversimplified attitude. The inner city slums are going to be around for a while and will remain high on the list of priorities for action in spite of the demographic trends.

Code enforcement

There is fairly general agreement on the desirability of establishing and enforcing adequate codes regulating the minimum standards of health, safety, and decency in residential buildings in the city. Usually this general agreement is followed by formidable buts. For this reason, very few cities have anything like full enforcement of housing codes. The principal reasons for this are the inherent difficulties and expense of housing codes, the political headaches engendered for an administration that decides on a code, and the fact that strict code enforcement would displace many slum residents.

The response to these difficulties must not be surrender, if a city is serious about arresting blight and improving its slum areas. Like everything else, code enforcement cannot stand alone. It must be one part, and an important part, of a comprehensive program to encourage conservation and rehabilitation of existing housing, strengthen the human beings in the slums, stimulate the construction of new low cost housing, increase employment opportunities, and take the profits out of substandard housing.

Some even go so far as to say that zoning, building, and housing codes are the basic tools for dealing with urban renewal problems.[6] This statement is overdrawn and reflects the antipathy of the authors to the intervention of the federal government in urban renewal problems (". . . there seems good ground to argue that abandonment of federal aid along with the related complicated procedures might be a net benefit" [7]), an antipathy obviously not shared by this book.

Where other elements of a broad anti-slum program are under way, then, a city administration should first review its housing codes to bring them in line with the best current thinking, and then establish a system of inspection and enforcement that will make them meaningful.

Some of the elements of an effective system are:

Adequate salaries for inspectors.

No unrealistically high and restrictive qualifications for the inspectors.

Frequent inspection of buildings most likely to fall below standard. All buildings cannot be inspected with the same frequency, nor need they be. It is obvious that some areas need more inspection than others and the frequency and intensity of inspection should be governed by these realities.

Consolidation of inspection services. Usually different departments inspect for fire hazards, health, construction defects, water, gas, and electricity. This results in waste of manpower, and confusion.

Simple, centralized records. Electronic data storage and retrieval systems offer great promise in this respect.

Better methods of scaling or grading violations should be installed so that priority attention can be given more serious violations.

More effective follow-up methods are required to insure correction of defects.

Flexible timing of inspections should be arranged so that owners or tenants are available during inspections.

The support and cooperation of the residents of a slum area in the inspection process and the follow-up should be sought. This area of citizen participation through neighborhood organizations has much room for developmnt. Not the least value of this is the nurturing of an *esprit de corps* that lends community pressure and approval to the physical improvement of the area.

Improvement of municipal services

Municipal services needing improvement are garbage collection, street and sidewalk maintenance, lighting, and care of parks and other public areas. This is another area in which an important contribution can be made without revolution, governmental reorganization, drastic new policy, or new bond issues. Municipal services are supposed to be provided uniformly throughout the jurisdiction. In most cities, they are not. The "better" areas get more attention.

Even uniform provision of municipal services throughout the city will not do the trick. What is needed is a reemphasis of this principle: services are to have uniform *effect* throughout the jurisdiction. In slum areas, more intense and expensive services are required just to maintain minimal standards.

Again, this alone will not turn the tide. In conjunction with other policies and actions, it is an important tool.

Taking the profits out of slum properties

This, like code enforcement, is a political hot potato, but one that cannot be dropped. Probably the most effective approach is through taxation that burdens the owner of slum properties in more realistic relationship to the return on the property. Likewise there usually can be a better balance between the weight of the tax on the land or site and the improvements on it. The tax should be in proper balance with the things that give true value. To give an impetus to conservation and rehabilitation, additional inducements through credits or deductions for investments that improve the property could be more widely and effectively employed.

Part of this effort, of course, is related to the enforcement of codes and regulations. The owners of substandard properties must not be allowed to get away with repeated violations. Low maintenance and repair costs are part of the equation that produces high profits on poor housing.

Tax delinquencies are another part. There are too many instances in which a property owner may be delinquent in tax payments, lose the property to the city, and then buy it back under conditions which in effect eradicate his tax obligation. Federal income tax depreciation deductions on slum properties or properties that do not comply with local housing or health codes should be eliminated.

New housing

Volumes have been written on this subject and it is impossible here to summarize or exhaust it or to offer new insights and suggestions. This is such an important topic, however, that there is need to mention some of the approaches relevant to the general argument of this book.

No proposals for improving slums can be complete without urging an increase in the stock of housing and the stocks available for low income familes. Although first priority in the inner city, for some time to come, must be given the conservation and renovation of structures that are basically sound but have been allowed to run down and get overcrowded, this needs to be complemented as part of long-term strategy by construction of new housing. A conservative estimate is that the present total housing production is at least 500,000 units short of our needs. During the 1960s about 16 millon new housing units will be required.

New housing is relevant to the slum in several ways. It makes older but good housing available through the trickle-down process. This can exert a positive influence on the average quality of housing *if* the older housing is not allowed to deteriorate and get overcrowded in the trickle down process. This is what is happening in many of the gray areas where higher income families have moved out, often into new housing in the suburbs, and the older houses left behind are occupied by lower income families. The older, larger houses often are cut into apartments or single rooms, the density per room goes up, the general tone of the neighborhood goes down, and the area is on the way to becoming a slum.

Much new housing in the city is middle income and luxury housing. There is nothing wrong with this, either, if it is accompanied by balanced attention to the housing needs of low income people. Middle income housing has been in short supply and has received legitimate encouragement through federal, state, and local government subsidy. There is a question now, however, as to emphasis. Even housing built by labor unions has been middle income housing. It is the view of this book that the emphasis on middle income housing should be eased and greater emphasis be given to housing for low income people.

Middle income housing has been emphasized for a number of valid reasons. After World War II, the building industry needed a boost and this was a logical sector of the market to focus on. Cities need the revenue represented by middle income families and it is good fiscal policy to foster construction of the kind of housing that will help to keep them in the city. In addition to this, if private capital is to be encouraged to build housing in the city, it is the middle and high income market that will be of interest, not the low income. The average price for new FHA-insured housing was nearly $15,000 per house in 1963.

There is difference of opinion as to how strong the government should be in continuing to subsidize the home-building industry. Some feel that FHA, for example, should operate at even higher levels of home value than it now does. Others feel that it is time for government to be more discriminating in its selection of targets and concentrate on the housing problems of the poor, the aged, and minority groups. Along with this should be federal and state government stimulus to the rational devolopment of metropolitan regions, with social, economic, and physical elements meshed to the greatest degree possible.

The time is ripe for stimulation of lower cost housing both within the city and in suburban areas. This, along with the promotion of integrated developmental processes, should be the main emphasis of governmental policy. Thus, under the heading of new housing construction, the emphasis is on new housing for low income people, but not for those at the bottom of the economic heap. More houses that sell for $10,000 or less and rental units of $100 per month or less are needed.

This implies direct and indirect intervention by government. First choice should be indirect supports and incentives, or bribes, if you will, to private builders to build low rent units, low cost multi-family units, and low cost houses. This means help with land acquisition, mortgage insurance at high loan-to-value ratios, favorable tax treatment—all the devices that can make the construction of housing at a level between public housing and middle income housing an attractive investment. This would also include encouragement of limited profit corporations or nonprofit corporations and cooperatives.

Levittown, New York, was an example of a move in this direction, although this was the result of the vigor and imagination of a builder without any special stimulus or aids from government. The Levittown houses represented a unique opportunity for many lower income families to buy outside of the city. It was made possible by the large scale of the operation and the application of mass production methods in on-site construction. Off-site prefabrication played only a small part.

The trouble with a lower income, suburban development

like Levittown is that it tends to become a class ghetto, homogeneous in aspect and restricted in the range of resident human types and indigenous culture. Where construction costs are so important in achieving a lower price for the final product, it is very difficult to overcome this homogeneity, and it is probably too much to hope that both objectives, low-priced housing and heterogeneous scattering, can be fully achieved. It is a goal not to be forgotten, however, and policy to promote that goal should be consciously fostered. Here we see again the old dilemma of policy makers: How many ends can be served at once? If many ends are not served, resolution of one problem may create new ones.

A strong role for the federal government is implied. First, the federal government has the credit tools necessary to skew the building industry in the direction of low cost housing. Second, some of this new construction should take place outside of the big city. The receiving areas are not going to take much initiative in this direction, in fact, they are more likely to resist it. Therefore, both state and federal governments must take the lead.

One thing to keep in mind here is the possibility of allowing local governments to purchase land outside their immediate borders for urban renewal. This has been done to some degree in England where local authorities have constructed housing "estates" in outlying areas. In the United States, state authorization and assistance would be required for this. It has far-reaching implications and would no doubt be politically difficult as it might be seen as an attempt of the central city to metropolitanize the area. Metropolitanizing, of course, has much to recommend it.

There is also room for some government building and

selling operations. They could be done directly, through a special-purpose federal authority, or by state or local authorities with strong federal financing. Any such operation should be self-supporting, if not at the outset, at least within a given period of time. The purpose is not to provide housing for people who can hardly afford any housing, but for those a cut above this. It is, in effect, to speed the movement up and out of people, rather than the filter-down process of old houses.

In this connection a strong case can be made for a program of direct federal loans (in contrast to the insurance of private loans). There are some markets that private capital just does not seem to be much interested in. Yet there is demand in terms of the need for adequate housing, even though the demand may not be "economic." Inner city housing for low income people is one of these markets. Fringe area housing is another one. Some cities near agricultural regions that have used migratory workers have developed shantytowns on their fringes. These, too, are slums and are not likely to disappear without help from government.

How much the private market will respond to bribes to build low income housing is an open question, and, until it is established that the response will be adequate, there is a legitimate role for pioneering government activity. This can be justified on the basis not only that more lower cost housing will be produced, but also that government would emphasize elements that private risk takers find it hard to do, such as fitting lower cost housing into broad community development plans and experimenting with new materials and building techniques.

Conservation and rehabilitation

Martin Meyerson states:

The most striking aspect of the housing market is the degree to which used houses outweigh new houses in importance. The vast stock of older houses constitutes 97 per cent of the supply in any year. . . . The stock of housing has been improved by the volume of new construction since the war, but in 1956 one of every five non-farm dwelling units was still dilapidated or lacking in basic facilities, and at least 2 million others were located in slums, industrial areas, or neighborhoods with poor public services. Still others were overcrowded or obsolete, or they suffered from little maintenance. However, by 1960 further improvements reduced the number of dilapidated units in the U.S. to 3 million from the 4.5 million in 1950.[8]

When used houses constitute so large a proportion of the total housing stock and when so many are in poor condition, logic demands a heavy emphasis on improving housing that already exists. This goes under the name of conservation and rehabilitation, and is currently receiving heightened attention in the housing and redevelopment business.

Experience has shown that, by and large, rehabilitation is less costly than new construction, and maintenance and conservation costs less than rehabilitation. There are approximately 7 million substandard housing units in the United States that could be rehabilitated. This is about the same as the number of families and individuals eligible for subsidized housing.

To stimulate the pace of conservation and rehabilitation in

run-down areas, both the carrot and the stick are required. The stick is enforcement of codes and informal community pressure. The carrot is help of various kinds from the public authorities.

This help can consist of financial aids, and technical assistance and drive. At present, the only significant special financial assistance for rehabilitation of privately owned housing is FHA mortgage insurance on loans contracted for rehabilitation of housing in officially designated urban renewal areas. There is room for expansion of this approach. In fact, large expansion will be required if the downhill race of deteriorating housing is to be significantly slowed and turned into an uphill climb. The pace to date has been much too slow. Speeding the pace would require designation of additional areas within which housing would be eligible for insured rehabilitation loans, and aggressive administration of a conservation and rehabilitation program within those areas including the upgrading of existing community facilities and provision of new ones to lend a tone of rebirth to the area as well as stepping up regular municipal services. The local government can help to induce action by owners through tax abatement for specific periods of time. Federal income tax deductions should be allowed for money spent on home improvement in areas designated as renewal or conservation areas in the city.

Beyond the provision of financial inducements, without which a "rehabilitation program" is not likely to get beyond the token or demonstration stage, technical assistance is needed. This means advice to the owner, resident or nonresident on the property, about financing, design for renovation work (rehabilitation can make an old building look like something out of a popular magazine, and this enhances value greatly), carpentry, plumbing, cement work, landscaping, painting, and so on.

Neighborhoods and areas designated for rehabilitation offer many opportunities for employment of youth on public work, thus getting at another aspect of the slum problem. Although rehabilitation on a house-by-house or building-by-building basis will no doubt make some progress, the progress is likely to be much faster if the rehabilitation effort is aimed at the entire neighborhood. The public aspects of this, such as repair of streets and sidewalks, making play or small park areas out of vacant lots, tree planting, building or renovating a community center or a school, can be done as part of a program sponsored by government or voluntary agency to provide employment and training for youth.

New Haven, Connecticut, where probably one of the most vigorous urban redevelopment programs in the country is being carried out, has had good experience with housing and neighborhood conservation. In the years between 1959 and 1963, 2,200 people (the total population is about 160,000) invested more than $6.6 million in rehabilitating their properties and the supply of standard dwellings was increased more than 21 per cent.

The New Haven program approaches conservation and rehabilitation with many tools: systematic area inspection, help with mortgage financing, help with planning improvements, effective enforcement of codes, quick action on complaints, homemaking education, special attention to key properties to inspire the neighbors, and publicity for people who have carried out attractive and effective improvements.

The following is an example of the financing on a one-family house in New Haven.

Original mortgage	$4,800 (5 years at 12 per cent)
Existing indebtedness	$2,400 (monthly payment, $106.77)
Cost of rehabilitation	$6,500
Total financing needs	$8,900
FHA mortgage approved	$9,700 (monthly payment, $57.66)

Rehabilitation accomplished: complete exterior repairs, installation of shutters, complete exterior painting, new porches, landscaping, repair of foundation and sidewalks, new furnace, new closets, new doors and windows, stairway repair, floor repair, new electrical wiring.

Not everyone is in favor of conserving and rehabilitating older housing. A leading spokesman for the opposite point of view is E. A. Gutkind. He says:

The city center has lost its intrinsic meaning. . . . City renewal, if it is not made part and parcel of a comprehensive reorganization of the whole structure of settlement on a large scale, is a phantasmagoria and will remain a self deception. . . . A centerless region (is) the next phase in the evolution of environmental structure. . . . Only large regional schemes and far reaching and systematic decentralization of the urban conglomeration can lead us out of the impasse.[9]

His prescription is that no slums be rebuilt. The old slum areas should be retained as open space so that the core of the metropolitan area will be thinned out. His ultimate picture shows scattered settlements, connected by rapid transit, separated by green belts, with some specialization among settlements and more people working in their own settlements rather than commuting to a central city.

No one can say that this dream is not true or that the

dire warning may not come to pass. Some will deny that the city center has lost its intrinsic meaning. There is little evidence that the big city center does not and will not continue to exert a powerful pull on people for business communication, recreation, cultural titillation, and just plain gregariousness. It seems probable that "spread city" as conceived by the New York Regional Plan Association [10] is a more realistic picture of the future.

For the pragmatic improver of the city a course that conserves and rehabilitates much old housing, builds some new low cost and middle cost housing in the inner city, and also provides for additional open space in between seems most promising.

President Johnson's message on housing, delivered to Congress on January 27, 1964, laid heavy emphasis on the use of existing housing. It recommended authorization of 50,000 additional public housing units in each of the next four years. Most of these would be new construction but some would represent rehabilitated existing structures. Some would even be leased.

Racial discrimination

Free housing choice for Negroes and other restricted minority groups will improve the physical quality of the housing stock. When Negroes can buy or rent a house or apartment wherever they want to, the demand for construction of new housing will increase, the market will be more fluid, and one of the reasons why slum housing is profitable—demand—will be eliminated. Therefore, any efforts in this direction will make a contribution toward the reduction of slums.

It would be a mistake to think that if racial discrimination in housing disappeared overnight, this would be followed immediately by an integrated housing pattern throughout metropolitan areas. For some time to come, many Negroes will want to live where there are other Negroes, and very often their preference may be to remain in the inner city if good housing is available. The fact that they have a choice and are not forced to occupy poor housing in a ghetto area will improve the housing available through the workings of the market. There is a long way to go in this matter. In the San Francisco Bay area in 1961, two thirds of the rental units were barred to Negroes.[11]

Subsidized housing for low income families

The approach to public housing is changing and needs to be changed further. The main direction of the change is and should be in the direction of subsidizing the family that needs better housing, rather than subsidizing the housing.

The public housing program was begun during the depression years when an overriding consideration was the need to create employment. Public housing was one form of the public works program of the time. There were, in 1963, 525,000 units of federally subsidized housing sheltering 2.1 million people. This is about 1 per cent of the total housing stock.

In recent years the large housing projects have been criticized for their tendency to become racial and class ghettoes and to destroy neighborhood and community relationships, their physical unattractiveness, their juvenile delinquency, and urine stains in the elevators. This is all perfectly legitimate criticism, but has gone too far. The fact that they are providing better physical housing for many people is too often overlooked.

James Baldwin provides a moving example of some of the bitter and stinging things that can be said:

> The projects in Harlem are hated. They are hated almost as much as policemen and this is saying a great deal. And they are hated for the same reason: both reveal, unbearably, the real attitude of the white world, no matter how many liberal speeches are made, no matter how many lofty editorials are written, no matter how many civil rights commissions are set up.
>
> The projects are hideous, of course, there being a law, apparently respected throughout the world, that popular housing shall be as cheerless as a prison. They are lumped all over Harlem, colorless, bleak, high, and revolting. The wide windows look out on Harlem's invincible and indescribable squalor: the Park Avenue railroad tracks, around which, about forty years ago, the present dark community began; the unrehabilitated houses, bowed down, it would seem, under the great weight of frustration and bitterness they contain; the dark, the ominous school houses from which the child may emerge maimed, blinded, hooked, or enraged for life; and the churches, churches, block upon block of churches, niched in the walls like cannon in the walls of a fortress.[12]

The criticism is so widespread and intense in some areas that hapless housing authorities sometimes feel themselves forced to produce reports to counteract it. New York City's report, *A Clearer Focus,* is a recent example. This report dealt with twelve current myths:

Tenants in public housing do not get adequate protection against crime (Yes, they do, said the Authority. The housing police force is the 24th largest in the United States.)

The developments are full of problem families (No, they are not. Only 2½ per cent are problem families.)

The Authority demolishes buildings with no concern for the families it dislocates (They do not.)

The Authority destroys more apartments than it builds (They do not. As of the end of 1962 it had destroyed 66,248 and built 120,465.)

The Authority insists on building huge developments of standard design (It used to, but does not any more.)

The great majority of public housing tenants are on public assistance; or the Authority discriminates against public assistance families (11.7 per cent of the tenants are receiving public assistance and the Authority tries to scatter such families around.)

The Authority discriminates against Negroes and Puerto Ricans; or only Negroes and Puerto Ricans can get into public housing (Neither is true. It tries to achieve some balance against impossible odds; 42.7 per cent of tenants are white, 39.8 per cent Negro, 16.9 per cent Puerto Rican.)

The Authority is content merely to put up buildings and supply housing (It has 81 community centers in operation, 41 golden age programs, 94 preschool and school-age programs, 31 health stations, 13 clinics, 9 branch libraries.)

The tenants are over-supervised and over-regulated (There are some regulations, such as no cats and dogs, but mostly tenants enjoy the same privacy as tenants in private housing.)

The Authority does not provide any housing for the elderly (One out of six apartments is occupied by an elderly person or family. The ratio will go up to one in four.)

The Authority does not pay taxes. The city also loses taxes because of the deterioration in real estate values in areas surrounding its developments (In 1962 the Authority paid $6,-

540,000 in city taxes. Property values actually increase in surrounding areas.)

We don't need more public housing (325,000 families in New York City live in substandard housing; 150,000 families and 50,000 elderly individuals have incomes too low to rent private housing; the Authority receives 85,000 applications per year.) [13]

The trend is away from the monstrous project to smaller units and different housing for low income families. The counter-pressure against this trend is the economy of large projects. They produce more low cost housing units at lower cost than most other methods, although this cost is not as low as one might think. It is close to $20,000 per unit. Illustrative of this trend was the press release from the New York Regional Office of the Public Housing Administration, July 22, 1963:

> Mr. Hillman's review further revealed a trend in planning away from super-block concentration of hundreds of units to smaller groupings of apartment houses harmonizing with neighborhood architectural and social patterns, more attractive and less institutional in appearance, not easily identifiable apart from the neighborhood. (He) emphasized that . . . urban renewal is providing available sites for relocation in the same neighborhoods where the clearance operations were undertaken. Consequently, residents of such blighted areas are not forced to move to other neighborhoods, often distant from the social and recreational associations of many years standing.[14]

At this point, it is perhaps well to reiterate the theme succintly stated in *Architectural Forum:* "the problems of public housing boil down, basically, to meeting the problem of poverty." [15]

It has been pointed out that there is a shortage of good low cost housing and this needs to be met by direct strengthening of the market processes for the production of lower cost housing and by stimulating the conservation and rehabilitation of older housing.

There will have to be continued direct building on government account, but there needs to be wider provision of supplemental rent money or certificates for low income families who cannot afford decent housing at going rates. First moves in this direction under federal leadership have been taken for large families. Extension of the principle at more adequate levels is called for.

A minor war will develop on the question of who should be in charge of the program, "housing" or "welfare." The welfare department will point out that it is already paying rent for its families and knows how to do it. There will always have to be a means test for families whose rent is to be subsidized, so extension of the rent subsidization policy is merely an extension of the welfare function. The housing people will say that there is a stigma attached to "welfare" and that no matter how much you try to change the image and reality of welfare, it is a degrading and dependency-producing system. Therefore, rent subsidy should be a housing program, where other financial assistance is not needed by the family. The case of the housers is strong.

Another method that should be encouraged is the purchase and renovation of old houses by the public housing authority. Philadelphia has successfully experimented with such a program.

There are great advantages to the program: it can provide dwelling units for large low income families, units which the

Housing Authority now lacks. It is an answer to the nagging question of how to do away with public housing's institutional "look" and atmosphere. It is economical, in fact downright cheap, in the face of costs of new construction. And it contributes to neighborhood improvement by rehabilitating houses of poor quality.[16]

In the first phase of the Used House Program 40 units were purchased and renovated at a total outlay of $351,436, or an average of $8,864 (only in six instances did the cost exceed $10,000). This, compared with a cost of $18,000 to $19,000 per unit in a high rise project (for less living space) presents a favorable argument for this approach.

"Once a public housing unit, always a public housing unit" ain't necessarily so. A policy of selling some public housing units to tenants as their income rises should be pursued. This is not feasible for large projects, but as the program moves toward smaller scattered units and even individual houses, as in the case of the Used House Program, it becomes practicable. Such a policy will serve the triple purpose of continually adding to the stock of good housing, of providing housing for low income families, and of reducing the necessity for pushing them out of their homes when their incomes rise.

How public purchase or construction of new housing outside the core city can be accomplished is a knotty problem that should get frank and open debate. It is a political issue, and a realist will be pessimistic about the possibilities of moving very far and fast in this direction under present circumstances. However, there ought to be some experiments with this, leading toward the development of general policy.

Cities should be able to purchase land for new housing outside their own borders, or to purchase older housing for rehousing some of their lower income residents. If the city government itself is not to be allowed to do this, then a regional authority or the state should do it. The essential element, of course, would be the rehousing, in outlying areas, of low income residents of the inner city. This does not mean a mass of low income minority group inner city residents would flood the suburbs. Many of them will not want to go if they can get decent housing in the city. But some will, and the long-term movement should be hurried as a means of eliminating the inner city ghettoes and providing good housing for lower income families.

Planning

Back in the good old days of a few years ago, "planning" was magic. There was city planning, regional planning, area planning, and even a thing called the National Resources Planning Board. Currently, in many quarters, planning is a favorite whipping boy or is regarded with disillusionment engendered by an unfulfilled, misplaced faith. It should be neither. In our pluralistic, heterogeneous, mixed, self-contradictory, unpredictable society it cannot be the ultimate instrument for social progress. On the other hand, progress is impeded if we do not do some planning. It is difficult to be a planner in a society that is suspicious of planning and yet insists on it, but often rejects, or worse, does not even hear the recommendations of planners.

The objectives of physical planning are to determine future land use (residential, commercial, industrial, institutional); lay out transportation routes; establish standards for population density; locate public facilities; indicate the kind of urban renewal needed for each section of the city; establish priorities and timetables for action. Within the past few years, there has been an increasing recognition of the fact that planning for the physical layout and appearance of a city has in the past been carried out too much in a vacuum. Not enough account has been taken of social and economic factors, which are strong determinants of what finally happens in the city. Nowadays the physical planners, in their conventions, are devoting time to consideration of social factors, and social workers and social scientists are inviting physical planners to make speeches at their meetings. The twain are beginning to meet, but have far to go before they are working in a really integrated manner.

Robert Weaver described the urban planning process in these general terms:

> In the broadest sense the urban planning process represents the self-conscious attempt by men to order their environment so as to realize certain common goals and values. As such, it is concerned not merely with the rational allocation of resources, but more importantly, with the selection of the goals and values toward which those resources should be directed. As a result, urban planning is an important part of the process by which consensus is achieved in a democratic society.[17]

Weaver is a "houser" but also a social scientist with years of experience as well in social action as chairman of the NAACP. He sees clearly the interrelatedness of the human and physical factors in planning for urban development.

All the current programs of the Housing and Home Finance Administration now push strongly toward integrated and comprehensive planning as a framework for urban renewal and redevelopment action. This is in contrast to the earlier tendency (which still has to be counteracted) toward "projectitis "

Under the Housing Act of 1954, cities can get federal grants to assist the financing of planning for orderly growth and development in urban areas. This can include planning for mass transportation for an entire urban area. A local community must have a "workable program" before it can qualify for federal urban renewal assistance. A workable program has to satisfy seven criteria:

There must be adequate local codes and ordinances, effectively enforced, or a realistic prospect of achieving this without delay.

There must be an adequate administrative organization to carry out urban renewal.

There must be an analysis of blighted neighborhoods to determine the treatment needed (bulldozer, spot clearance, rehabilitation, conservation, and so on).

There must be a comprehensive plan for the development of the community.

The local community must be able to meet the financial obligations of a renewal plan.

There must be an adequate plan for relocating the families displaced by the destruction of old housing.

The plan must have been prepared with active citizen participation.

This is a difficult list of requirements. In order to get on with the job, it has been necessary for the federal Urban Renewal Administration to accept workable programs varying widely in quality. The planning process would be assisted if H.H.F.A. could make annual renewal grants on a programmed basis to cities with comprehensive redevelopment plans, rather than making grants on a project-by-project basis.

The Community Renewal Program, which came into being in 1959, carries the workable program further toward the goal of a comprehensive and coordinated approach to urban renewal needs by identifying and measuring, in broad terms, the total need for urban renewal in the community, relating this need to the resources available in the community, and developing a long-range program for carrying out urban renewal activities. It is not requisite that a city have a community renewal program in order to receive federal urban renewal assistance, but it is encouraged. Federal grants (not to exceed two-thirds of the cost) can be secured for developing such programs.

The Community Renewal Program affords an opportunity to consider correction of the economic and social aspects of blight as well as the physical aspect. It also can expose problems beyond the means of the local community to solve and can look beyond the borders of the city, in analyzing the problem and making recommendations.

Although the C.R.P. idea is one of the most promising events on the planning scene in recent years and is bound to exert pressures toward more meaningful planning for the city, there are still formidable obstacles to achieving maximum effectiveness. A group of experts on the subject, meeting to review the first three years of experience, listed the primary obstacles:

Fragmented governmental structure that creates intergovernmental competition and prevents solution of certain problems.

High re-use appraisals that discourage the interest of private developers in renewal areas.

High turnover of governmental personnel, which breaks continuity of understanding.

Bureaucratic jealousies in and among governmental agencies that block effective coordination of action.

Difficulties in conveying to the decision makers the complex considerations of a community renewal program.[18]

One of the sharpest critics of planning and planners today, Jane Jacobs, has practically nothing nice to say about them in their present guise, but she is far from against planning itself. It is easy to get the impression from her book, *The Death and Life of Great American Cities*,[19] that she disapproves of planning. This is not true. She just does not like the way planners have behaved up to the present time. One of her major points is that without a high degree of diversity within neighborhoods and areas in the city it is impossible to preserve and promote the physical, social, and economic vitality that is necessary to make the inner city a viable place. She feels that professional planners have been going directly counter to this by their insistence on doing away with mixed-land use, bulldozing old structures unnecessarily, straightening and widening streets, trying to reduce densities, and the like. She makes a strong case for just the opposite: mixed land use, small blocks, preservation of older buildings, high population density, irregular and short streets. With specific reference to slums, she advocates what she calls unslumming: making slum neighborhoods attractive enough to draw or keep residents who could afford to live elsewhere.

For certain areas, this is highly desirable, and certainly there are strong pressures in planning and in urban renewal policies leading in this direction. These tendencies should be encouraged. Mrs. Jacobs relies too heavily on diversification as the major principle in the attack on slums. She denounces the authors of ideas she does not like, such as the city beautiful and garden city, as peddlers of panaceas, but she herself can be accused of the same disease, in going overboard for diversification. Let us have diversification but do not think it is going to cure the ills of the slum. It is an important goal in dealing with the physical environment, nonetheless. To achieve it will require strong central planning and control on the part of the city government.

It is impossible to present a neat formula for the shape and content of a city's planning effort. There are extraordinary complications in trying to take account of the many forces determining the nature of the city and forming its slums. In a society organized as ours is and embodying principles of free choice and private decision-making, planners are faced with many imponderables of human behavior. They are also fenced in by the limitations on the capacity of government to impose its plan on a community, any important segment of which is strongly resistant. Some important generalizations should be taken into account, however.

Planning for the physical environment of the city should be as comprehensive as possible in two directions, subject matter and geography. It should be based to the greatest extent possible on analysis of and predictions about all the physical, demographic, economic, social, educational, and governmental factors that influence urban development and it should apply to as wide a relevant geographic area as possible.

It should be carried out close to where decisions are made. Too many plans have been academic exercises not really useful for local legislators and administrators.

There is no fixed plan valid for all time. A plan must be capable of change to take account of changing conditions and must have built into it procedures for facilitating that change.

A plan should have both short-term and long-range aspects, so that ultimate goals are spelled out as far as possible and at the same time there are guides for digestible parts of the long-range plan.

A plan should be supported by extensive information and projections, and various possible choices should be indicated. With these characteristics it should be useful to private and public decision makers alike.

Planning should be carried out so that it is more than a technical exercise by professional experts; it should strive to be what Robert Weaver hopes for, "an important part of the process by which consensus is achieved in a democratic society."

A number of cities since 1962 have been developing new approaches to planning and action on social problems. Notable among these are Boston (Action for Boston Community Development), Philadelphia (Philadelphia Council for Community Advancement) New Haven, Connecticut (Community Progress, Inc.) and Washington D.C. (United Planning Organization). These cities, with the help of the Ford Foundation, organized nonprofit corporations with representation from public and private sectors to analyze the crucial problems of their slums and gray areas, plan and promote action on them, help to finance the action, and evaluate the results. Federal agencies have also made grants through these organizations. Principal among these have been the President's Committee on Juvenile Delinquency and Youth Crime, the National Institute of Mental Health, and the Office of Manpower, Automation, and Training, of the Department of Labor.

The hope has been that these instrumentalities would have the following characteristics, new to the usual city scene:

—the capacity and willingness to see the community and its problems whole rather than as a collection of agencies and self-interests;

—the capacity to set common goals, to fix priorities, to develop new approaches, to test them in action, and to evaluate performance against national rather than local standards only;

—the capacity to mobilize governmental as well as private resources, and to forge working relationships among agencies of both sectors; the capacity to involve and to affect critical centers of community power, including the intellectual, in order to break the bottlenecks in education, employment, law, health, and other fields;

—the capacity to finance the considerable costs of research and experimentation and, afterwards, of continuing programs which experimentation has proved worthwhile, in the growing conviction that governmental budgets will more and more have to carry the main burden of community services and that private agencies will emphasize the critical, the evaluative, and the experimental;

—the capacity to convince the people involved—on one level, the industrial, labor, governmental, and civic leadership, and on another level, the man in the Grey Area street—that these programs are 'for real'—not window-dressing for the *status quo,* not a crumb dropped conspicuously by the affluent few who dine at the community's main table.[20]

A number of cities have received grants from the President's Committee on Juvenile Delinquency to plan and demonstrate comprehensive juvenile delinquency programs which involve a variety of public and private agencies.

Paying the bill

This is an increasingly interconnected and interdependent society. The man who lives in the suburbs has a stake in the inner city either as his place of work, play, or cultural enrichment, or as the source of burdens or costs which in part ultimately fall on him. He may have to help pay for a criminal from the slum in a state or federal prison. He has to help support state mental health facilities which house a disproportionate number of poor people. He pays for public assistance recipients through state and federal taxation. The list is long. It behooves him therefore to be ready to share the financial burden of upgrading the inner city if for no other reason than to reduce the ultimate costs of failing to upgrade it.

The cities themselves cannot pay the total bill for the human and physical renewal and development discussed in this book. State and federal governments have greater resources and generally utilize types of taxation that spread across the population more equitably than does the property tax, which is still the mainstay of municipal finance.

It is reasonable to expect that in the future there will be merging of special districts, such as school or fire, so that the wealthier ones can help finance the poorer ones. There will also be increases in state and federal subsidies to localities for special purposes. Neither of these should be resisted. Both should be encouraged. Along with this is likely to be further city use of the payroll tax and other taxes that identify the true sources of wealth and tax them appropriately.

Such a brief reference to this subject obviously avoids its great range of complexities. Much more needs to be said than just that the state and federal governments should assist the city with more money than they now do, although this is a central principle. Beyond this is the need for identifying the most efficient and effective level or area from which to draw taxes so the burden is equitable, and at which to administer particular services. This is needed in order to arrive at some rational basis for conscious transfer payments between levels of government.

Other approaches focus on particular types of payment that hit the inner city particularly hard, such as welfare payments. Should these be transferred to the county or financed by the state? What would be the results of each in equity and efficiency? How about streets and roads? Of how much value is a downtown street to a resident of suburbia and how much and how should he be asked to pay for it? These and other elements present difficult problems in politics, equity, and technique. They all must be considered in the context of the metropolitan region.

CHAPTER VII

Social and
Health
Services

T HE PRECEDING section noted that in the past, one common and oversimplified view of the slums held that the solution to its problems lay in slum clearance and housing. Another parallel and equally myopic view gave the answer as more and better social services.

Obviously, neither of these perspectives is all wrong. Indeed, there is a lot of right in them. The danger lies in either one being embraced exclusively. Each has an important place but not the important place. There is danger in the tendency to think that the lasting solutions lie in rehabilitating people or in "helping people in trouble." The lasting solutions lie in arranging our social and economic institutions and systems so that there are opportunities for all to work, to have adequate income, to participate in social relationships that are not hurtful or destructive, to be a part of a larger society, and in improving the institutions that prepare people to fill these roles.

The answers do not lie primarily in rehabilitating the young unwed mother, or the delinquent boy, or the skid-row alcoholic, or the demoralized, deserting father. Our society will never work well enough and our interpersonal relationships will never be universally healthy enough so that no one will need individual help and rehabilitation. Such services will always be necessary and should be made available to all people, rich and poor alike, on a competent and professional basis. But let no one mistakenly believe that in such services lies prevention of the problem of the slums.

Social work is not limited to helping people in trouble. Social workers staff services to ordinary groups, settlement houses, and neighborhood centers. They operate the social or community planning councils that plan for health and welfare services as well as the community funds that finance, in part, the voluntary agencies.

Unfortunately it has often been popularly thought—and social workers have allowed and even encouraged this misapprehension—that the resolution of the problems of slum people lies in the provision of more and better social welfare services. This has had two unsought effects: it diverted attention and thought from better analysis and prescriptions for the problems of poverty, personal malfunctioning, dependency, deviancy, and slums; and it made social work carry an undeserved stigma of ineffectiveness and failure in the face of rising delinquency rates, heavy public assistance rolls, increasing illegitimacy, increasing family breakdown, and the continued existence of vast acres of slums. Social work has enough difficulty showing results within its legitimate area of operations, without being charged with the failure to remedy the inadequate functioning of the basic institutions of our society.

Social work has allowed this misapprehension to develop for several reasons. First is the history of the profession. The first social work took place in response to the needs of the poor. On an increasingly organized basis, it ministered to the poor, the sick, and the homeless. At first it was entirely voluntary. It was not until 1883 that public social security systems began to be established in Europe to meet the minimum financial needs of certain eligible categories of people. Social security did not become a part of the American scene until the depression of the 1930s. To their credit, social workers were in the forefront of the drive to establish a national social security system in America and they drafted the basic legislation. They also invented the federal-state-local cooperative system of public assistance which during the depression was addressed to all in need. Toward the end of the depression, federal contributions to general relief were eliminated. Since then, the federal government has contributed only to direct financial assistance for certain categories of the needy: the aged, dependent children (in 1962 changed to families of dependent children), the blind, and the disabled. In other words, eligibility for relief stems from some obvious individual characteristic that accounts for the dependency. Unemployment or poverty, for some unidentifiable or uncategorizable reason, are not among such qualifying characteristics.

To those working closely with the poor and the malfunctioning or nonfunctioning, it is apparent that relief, shelter, or a friendly visit are not enough to change the basic condition of the individual or to change his behavior. In response to this awareness one can look inward, in the person and intimate family relationships, for causative factors, or look to the workings of the societal structure to locate the distortions, uneven

pressures, and frustrations that influence the status, performance, and capacity of individuals.

In any particular case one must obviously look in both
directions. In analyzing the position of large segments of the
population whose position is inferior, such as Negroes, the
poor, juvenile delinquents, or migrants, the social, cultural, and
economic context within which the group exists is more relevant for analysis. The practitioners of social work have tended
to overemphasize the personal, individual, and familial matrix
to the neglect of the socioeconomic and cultural.

There is a perfectly understandable reason for this. During
the period of the most intense and rapid development of social
work as a profession, when graduate schools of social work
were being established and professional qualifications for
agency personnel promoted, there was a flowering of knowledge about human personality and behavior. This was given
initial impulse by Freud and deepened, elaborated, and modified by his successors and intellectual competitors. These men
brought to the world new understandings of the influences of
early childhood experiences and familial relationships on
human feelings and behavior, and new understanding of the
powerful workings of the subconscious.

This knowledge was so inspiring, so challenging, and so
relevant to the understanding of certain aspects of the human
behavior with which social workers were faced that the profession made it the core of the practice of social work. This
meant that attention was diverted from the social context.
There would be nothing to complain about if this had not
happened.

Social work became less and less involved with the problems of the poor and thus of the slums. People's psyches could
not be dealt with unless they themselves were ready to look

inward, with the help of a case worker. The poor tend to be so beset with the concrete problems of existing that they are usually not inclined or able to indulge in introspection. Likewise, the lower class culture doesn't support this kind of orientation. Lower class people tend to look outside themselves for the reason when something goes wrong. It was bad luck, or fated, or "they" did it. Thus the predominant treatment method of social welfare agencies was not suited to the individuals in the slum. There has been a degree of disengagement of the social work from the poor.

Let it be said that these comments refer to general characteristics and trends. The picture is not black and white. The situation has been painted in broad strokes and there are significant exceptions. The color and form of the broad strokes, however, are difficult to deny.

A high official of the National Association of Social Workers has suggested that there may, in fact, be two professions mixed up in what is called one: a profession that serves and treats clients, and another that attempts to bring about social change.[1] It may be that the first profession has become highly developed somewhat at the expense of the other.

There is an increasing awareness of the situation described above among some leaders of the profession, and energetic efforts to redirect attention to social problems are under way. A few quotations illustrate this.

> We are dealing too much with residual problems. We need to break through to get better management of social problems and better intervention when and where it can make a difference.[2]

> There are periods when social problems have reached a magnitude that makes the gap between practice and avowed goals highly visible. We are in such a period now. There is no ques-

tion that social work must study, diagnose, and "treat" its own approaches if it is to make a contribution toward the modifications in social relationships necessary for a period of scientific revolution.[3]

We have become too much of a technical service, focusing on deep-dish therapy, based on borrowed concepts, divorced from the culture in which we live which is doing more to people than their psychic maladjustments.[4]

We must not permit our social welfare institutions to remain aloof from these great social and economic changes of our time. We must not exhibit a tendency to make social work irrelevant to these issues, and to prefer it that way. We must not become overly immersed in rehabilitative activities, or lead the public to believe that rehabilitative strategies are adequate to the solution of the problems found in a changing world.[5]

The second major reason why social work has allowed and perhaps fostered the misapprehension that the resolution of the problems of slum people lies in the provision of more and better social welfare services is that the social agencies have to raise money from the community. This is true primarily for voluntary agencies dependent on contributions, but it also applies to public agencies, since their funds have to be provided by legislators who respond to the same stimuli as voluntary contributors. It is much easier to raise money by soliciting it to "help the poor" even though this sometimes slightly stretches the truth. Tear-jerking appeals remain the most effective and are very difficult for the agencies to abandon. Therefore, the public can only conclude from the fund-raising literature and posters that the overwhelming concern of social agencies is with the problems of the poor. Unfortunately, a

number of reliable studies have shown that the clientele of most
social agencies has become increasingly middle class and middle
income. There is an illusion of service to the poor of which
the agencies themselves may be victims.

Is there an important role for social service agencies, and
particularly voluntary ones, in the slums? If so, how can they
best function? This discussion relates to social services such
as family counseling, case-work services of various kinds, group
work, neighborhood centers, settlement houses, and the like.
It does not relate to public assistance. The answer to the question is that social services are important in the array of weapons
needed for the attack on slum problems, and private agencies
have a significant role to play.

The heaviest investment of the community should be in
those basic institutions and systems and strategies that will
prevent later human wreckage. There will always be those,
however, who need individual counseling in coping with whatever problems may be besetting them. This need is not governed
by income level, although the problems of the poor are multiplied by their penury and given a different quality. Likewise,
there is a wide field for social service activity with groups of
all ages and types in the slums.

Some of the ways of working and organizing that will help
social welfare agencies reach into the real problems of the
slums and reach the people of the slums are outlined in the
following sections.

Operating near the problems

Many people who may turn to a professional agency for help if it is handy will not do so if a long trek downtown is required. If agencies want only highly motivated people to come to them for help, one way to keep the under-motivated away is to be physically distant. However, if agencies are better to meet the needs of slum people, they must deal with under-motivation. Therefore, they must make themselves available in local offices, even of the store-front variety, near the people.

One approach to this was mentioned earlier in connection with the community school. Some social agencies could establish outpost personnel or small offices in or associated with the community school, as is the plan in Detroit.[6]

An alternative is the supermarket approach—the location under one roof of a number of agencies and departments. This brings the services closer to the people and has the added virtue of fostering integrated effort by a variety of agencies. The way agencies have defined themselves and divided the labor among themselves arises from logical analysis and historical accident, so that one agency provides family counseling, another adoption services, another legal counsel, another health services for adults, and so on. The problems of people in need unfortunately do not divide up so neatly. One family may need all of the kinds of specialized services listed above at any one time and they do not care much which agency they get them from.

One of the classical problems in welfare administration has been the fragmentation of services and the ineffective working of referral systems. A mother may seek help from Legal Aid in staving off the bill collector for the installments on the television set. During the course of the interview the attorney may discover that the reason she has no money is that her husband is ill at home without medical care and without income, or that he has just deserted the family. The older boy may be in trouble with the police, the teen-age daughter may be pregnant out of wedlock, and there may be a mentally defective child in the home who has to be cared for constantly. All of these separate problems are just one big problem for the mother. As far as she is concerned they are inseparable and each one aggravates the others. This is the "multi-problem family."

Even if the problems are not so many, there are likely to be at least a couple of things that need attention. They can be better attended to if a referral can be made just down the hall, instead of several miles away.

Some of the services needed by people are highly complex, such as legal aid in securing support payments. Others are quite simple. A service center in a slum area should be prepared to offer a wide range of services from the simplest provision of information to complicated legal or case-work services. Among the common needs of slum residents is elementary information about the city—where to go to pay a gas bill, whom to go to see about a truancy report, what to do about a traffic ticket, how to get to the immigration office, where to get a polio shot, whom to complain to about rats, what to do about water leaking. Often little problems become big problems just for lack of information.

In addition to the value of providing such information to people who are sophisticated about certain aspects of life in the slum jungle but surprisingly naïve about other aspects, there is an added reward. Such a neighborhood or district service center should be known as more than just a place to go with a big problem. It should be known as an information center as well as a problem-solving center. When you are seen there by your neighbors it does not necessarily mean that you have a big problem you cannot solve yourself. It may mean that you are just going in for some simple information. This thus makes it easier for you to go in without stigma. Experiments along these lines are being conducted in several of the larger cities.

As part of the delinquency prevention program on the lower East Side of New York the Mobilization for Youth Program has established three neighborhood service centers in a population area of just over 100,000. These have the following goals:

To provide a wide range of information about community resources, from the school system to the subway system.

To teach skills in such matters as budget management, purchasing, home management, and child care.

To act as intermediaries in dealings with bureaucratized services and institutions.

To establish close connections among area, district, and city-wide resources; to ensure the coordination of Mobilization for Youth and other institutional services.

To offer such direct services as nurses, baby sitters, homemakers, and escorts, in order that the burdens of lower income living may be eased and that educational, vocational, medical, and other community services may be used more fully.

To offer enabling social resources with professional sensitivity and psychological insight so that they may be most effectively used.

To offer immediate help in time of trouble or emotional distress—"emergency psychological first aid."

To make available intensive diagnosis and treatment services to selected low income persons.

To accomplish all this the Neighborhood Services Centers offer inquiry, liaison-resources, "under-the-roof," social planning, referral, and reintegration services. Representatives of various municipal departments, such as housing, welfare, and health, are stationed in the centers as are employment services. Legal Aid Society attorneys and full-time case workers for liaison with the courts are also there.

In Pittsburgh, plans are being made to establish a neighborhood service agency in the Homewood-Brushton area. It will be called the Community Services Association (COMSERVE). The purposes of COMSERVE are to be:

—to coordinate the variety of services, originating inside and outside of Homewood-Brushton, which are available to local residents, in order to insure their most effective application and utilization;

—to stimulate the interest and intervention of outside resources in the problems of Homewood-Brushton through persuasion or through the use of financial incentives such as the purchase of new services on a demonstration basis;

—to demonstrate new services which are needed to solve problems with which existing services cannot adequately cope and which are not the current responsibility of an existing agency.[7]

COMSERVE has objectives beyond the providing of coordinated or integrated social services in the area of need. It also will play the role of community organizer, program stimulator, and service innovator. It will be the organizational leader for a total community plan, and will provide funds to get the new services started, not necessarily under its own direction.

In Chicago a recommendation has been made for the establishment of a Social and Health Services Center in the East Woodlawn area, just south of the University of Chicago.

This center would provide referral information and guidance, as well as a variety of short term services, directly under one roof, for a wide range of social, economic, legal, and medical problems. It would serve as a readily accessible center for people with emergency or immediate needs for help with the problems of pressing social reality. A major function of staff would be to provide referral service and to assure that persons needing services were effectively connected with other service programs. Also efforts to develop high quality short duration treatment programs would permit existing service resources in the area to deal more effectively with long term problem situations.

Such a service center would ideally include representatives of the following types of agencies: Board of Health, Planned Parenthood Association, Family Service Bureau, United Charities, Cook County Bureau of Public Aid, Illinois State Employment Service, Housing Department, Board of Education, and the Police Department. Wherever possible these existing agencies, public and voluntary, should be encouraged to assign service personnel to the center, who will be empowered to function both in relation to specific agency objectives, but also in relation to an experimental plan of coordinated services directed to the "total" welfare of clients. Where needed and feasible, and not available through existing agencies, new types of services and personnel should be developed. Undoubtedly new conceptualizations of service patterns, and their creative implementation, will have to be developed within the framework of such a center.[8]

Concrete services

The private welfare agencies with the most highly qualified personnel have more and more limited themselves to deep psychological treatment of clients troubled by emotional problems and family stress. These people may also be burdened by environmental problems, but the main focus of the agency operation is counseling, guidance, and relationship therapy with a view to strengthening the individual so that he can better cope with his problems or his disturbance himself.

As pointed out earlier, this method does not work very well with low income families and individuals. This apparently is partly because lower class ways of living do not equip them to participate readily in a process that requires one to verbalize, to ruminate introspectively, and to look within the personality for ways to grow and to readjust and to cope. For many people in low income areas, this case work method seems to be unrealistic.

Most people in the slums who may use the services of a private welfare agency are so beset with immediate, pressing, and very objective and external problems that dealing with their emotional problems or inadequacies does not seem very relevant. They have been described as leading lives of quiet desperation. Sometimes the desperation is not so quiet. They feel they need help with what seem to them to be the causes of the desperation. The life of low income people has also been described as moving from one crisis to another and this is not an inaccurate description. The poor need help with the crises, and when they ask for it they need it right now!

Case work agencies that wish to function more effectively in the slums will have to adjust themselves to these realities.

This sounds very much like an anthropologist's treatise on the culture of the natives on some isolated island, of which the missionaries will have to take account. The parallels are very close.

In a low income area, case work agencies must combine their skills in helping people to modify individual behavior and attitudes with systematic efforts to change their social and economic circumstances. Many problems are not exclusively attributable to defects in the environment or to defects in individual response to the environment. These are interacting and mutually reinforcing elements and both must be worked on. Private case work agencies have tended to take too little account of the environmental factors in recent years. This calls for greater provision of concrete services to change and relieve environmental pressures that may be impairing the individual's capacity to function.

Methods of intake, diagnosis, and treatment

Frank Riessman, psychologist on the staff of Mobilization for Youth and research associate with the Columbia University Department of Psychiatry, has studied how traditional case work techniques can be modified to accommodate low income clients. A twofold strategy is called for in this respect: the modification of techniques by the social work profession, and the conscious preparation of the low income client for aspects of treatment which he is not expecting.[9] The following suggestions borrow heavily from Reissman:

Keep interviews informal, with not too much note writing. Don't be afraid of humor.

Let the client unload bitterness. Do not fear being forceful. Give some service right away.

Do not diagnose with middle class standards. Learn the idiom of the low income client, but do not falsely use it.

Treatment may take place in unusual places. The case worker may attend a family celebration, accompany the father to his place of work, meet him at the corner bar, talk to a boy sitting in a truck, or walk around pushing the baby carriage with the mother. A natural setting removes some of the fears the client may build up in a strange office.

The worker should not pretend to be something he is not. Do not manipulate or lie to the client—nothing is likely to happen if genuine concern is not felt and expressed by the worker, but this should not become indulgence. The consequences of negative behavior (e.g., drug addiction) should be clearly and truthfully discussed.

Capitalize on the fact that the psychological difficulties of an individual often diminish in importance when the individual becomes involved in some demanding commitment outside of himself, such as a religious movement, hobby, a social movement. Many low income clients today are members of some minority group. Involvement in the movements to improve the social, political, and economic position of these groups may have strong therapeutic efforts for an individual. This does not mean pressuring low income clients to get on a picket line, but it does mean encouragement would be in order, since these movements after all are aimed at correcting some of the basic conditions which are part of the low income client's ailment. Participation in such movements also identifies the client with something important beyond himself, and may give him a feeling of power and of being somebody, in contrast to most of the other conditions of his life which are telling him that he is nobody. Regardless of what one might think of the Black Muslim movement, it has had just this effect for a great many people. Unquestionably there are dangers in this involvement approach, but perhaps it is time to err in new directions. Involvement in creative artistic activities or scientific work may represent other indirect routes to affecting what has been seen in the first instance as "the problem" of the individual.

Let it be known that it is all right and useful to express personal feelings to a professional who is not a priest or minister, that miracles cannot be expected and that change takes time, that talk itself can be useful, that change takes work and can not come just from the outside, that some difficulties are produced by defensiveness, transference, and the like, that some physical ailments can be in part psychologically caused, that one can criticize and yet love and respect one's family.

These suggested modifications of case work practice are all in the direction of facilitating rapport and communication between professional social workers, who are highly educated and come from middle class backgrounds, and low income, low status, or lower class clients. Lack of communication has been one of the major obstacles to effective operation of social agencies that use traditional case work methods in slum areas. Also suggested are approaches to treatment that have a better chance of directly or indirectly influencing the situation and behavior of low income clients in contrast to those of higher social and economic status.

Use of nonprofessional personnel

There are two major aspects of this theme. One is the chronic shortage of professionally trained social workers, with no indication that this situation is going to change in the near future. In order for welfare agencies to do the big job confronting them, they must learn which social work tasks can be performed by people without professional training.

The second aspect of the use of nonprofessional personnel, volunteer or paid, applies specifically to the low income community. Many people whose origins are in the low income community, or who are still there, may sometimes communicate more effectively with others of like background better than a professionally trained worker. They are often able to understand (or at least "feel") the situation, attitudes, and ways of thinking of slum residents better than those who have not had this experience or are not now part of it. After all, the slum resident has been "trained" in it. It cannot be assumed automatically that all poor people, or people from lower class backgrounds, have this capacity. Some who started in the slums and left have turned their back on their origins with a vengeance. Nevertheless, many people still resident in the slums, carefully selected, can perform a number of tasks in social agencies, as well as other institutions functioning in the slums, and can be of great influence on their peers. They may in fact be able to accomplish certain objectives better than professionally trained personnel whose personal milieu is the middle class world.

Several illustrations will clarify the point. Women residents of Chicago, who have come from the southern Appalachian mountains, are on duty with Travelers' Aid at the bus depot to assist newly arriving people from that area. The southern Appalachians are a depressed area from which many rural white people have migrated north, chiefly to Cincinnati, Columbus, Cleveland, Detroit, Chicago, and other cities in the upper midwest. In Chicago there is a large concentration of these migrants on the near North Side. They have come from a rural background and a culture in many ways distinctive. Even their language is distinctive. Someone to meet such people, who, bewildered, short of money, ignorant of the big city, can be of great assistance in their initial adjustment to the city. If that someone understands their language and their ways and is one of them, and, to boot, knows something about the city and its resources, the help is multiplied.

Teen-age boys, who like cars and like adventure, operate road patrols on the highways converging on Chicago, looking for southern migrants whose old cars may have broken down or who otherwise may need help on the highway. Some of these boys have records of delinquency.

Men and women from low income areas work as paid or volunteer staff with the public school to stimulate closer connections between school and community.

Gang leaders are employed as field assistants or consultants in the Chicago YMCA detached worker program. Former youthful offenders are employed by the New York State Division for Youth in interviewing and other research related tasks.

Homemakers are becoming an increasingly important service performed by social agencies in low income areas. These are often women from similar areas. Street-corner workers, detached workers, or extension workers of certain kinds can be older teen-agers or young adults from low income backgrounds.

High school students who are doing well in school have been successfully employed as tutors for younger elementary or high school pupils. College students from middle class or lower class backgrounds can act as tutors or project leaders. Both high school students and college students in such roles serve as models of success for the youngsters with whom they are in contact.

Indigenous leaders are used for community organization work in the local area, as are indigenous assistants for a wide variety of group activity with youngsters.

Unmarried mothers assist in day care facilities or health care centers where their own children may be involved. Teen-age girls can also help in day care centers. The girls will be exposed at the same time to considerable education about child care, family life, and family planning.

Residents of the slum area who are employed can be used in vocational guidance on a neighborhood basis.

Former tuberculosis patients are recruited as investigators to make home visits and follow-ups on patients. Prisoners can serve as "friendly visitors," case aides, and volunteers in health services and services for the aged. This is being done in Wandsworth Prison in London.

These are but a few examples of how residents of low income areas with minimal education can be used to improve the social services of the area. Needless to say, such personnel must be carefully selected. They also must be carefully supervised and trained on the job. With these provisions, however, they have the potential to make strong contributions to the effectiveness of the social services. Herbert Gans has clearly stated the issue:

> Since it is doubtful that middle-class professionals can soon develop the knowledge and empathy needed to communicate with lower-class clients, it may be necessary to dichotomize these professions, assigning professionals to develop the programs, and recruiting skilled non-professionals to adapt them to lower-class clients and carry them out. These non-professionals should be people who have themselves come out of lower-class culture, and have successfully moved into a more stable way of life—either working or middle class—but have not rejected their past. Many mobile people tend to turn their backs on the culture from which they have come, and become more hostile toward it than anyone else. Yet, there are some people who, in making the change, have developed a considerable amount of empathy toward both the old and the new culture. Since they know the conditions and the culture that are to be changed, and the way of life that is being sought by and for lower-class clients they should be more successful in achieving rapport with such clients than are middle-class professionals. But while these empathic people exist in large numbers, they are hard to find. Some have been drawn into settlement houses and into group work with adolescent gangs. Most of them, however, probably earn their living in factories and offices, without ever using their talent—for it is a talent—to mediate between the classes.[10]

Participation of the low
income community in
agency decision making

A survey of the East Woodlawn area in Chicago noted that the local branch of the Family Service Bureau of the United Charities of Chicago was regarded by the residents of the area as "their" organization. Notable about this statement was the necessity to make it. It was a high compliment to this agency. The ordinary social agency is not so regarded by the indigenous residents of a slum area; it is seen as an institution representing "them." Sometimes it is accepted in a friendly fashion, sometimes with indifference, sometimes with outright hostility. Sometimes it is dismissed as a bunch of do-gooders, sometimes as people who are busying themselves with pursuits that nobody understands very well but "if they don't bother anybody leave 'em alone." Sometimes they are seen as representing the charity handout of rich people to salve their consciences and keep the poor people quiet and out of sight.

When the local poor community feels isolated from an agency that is supposed to be helping it, that agency's job is rendered that much less effective. There are ways of overcoming this, at least to some extent.

Although private agencies will have to continue to get their financial support from the wealthier part of the community (and subventions from public funds) they can experiment with ways of soliciting the participation of representatives of the low income community at various levels of decision-making. It is even possible to raise money in the low income community through cake sales, parties and picnics, special events, and the like. This, too, will give the area a feeling of sponsorship of the agency and make its representatives more welcome in the area.

More blue collar people should be on agency boards and committees. Lip service is paid to this principle every now and then, but the instances in which it has been put into practice are rare. If an agency is city-wide in coverage, it should have blue collar representation on its city-wide board. It should also have neighborhood or district committees heavily representative of working and lower class groups, for its work in low income areas. *Ad hoc* involvement of indigenous residents to help plan a specific short-term local activity or new program would have a long-term goal of integration of the agency in the local area.

Relation of social services to other institutions in the slums

It is clear from the general argument of this book that no one institution, or agency, or program, or policy, or course of action, is sufficient in itself against the magnitude of the problems of the slums. This is true, of course, for social service agencies. It is the function of the social agencies to sustain people who are incompetent and out-of-it, to mend people who can again be whole, and get back into it, and to help people who are threatened with being pushed out of it to hang on.

It takes powerful performance to be successful at this, and it takes the combined strength of all the institutions whose function it is to build human beings or to stem the tide of disintegration. This means that social agencies that propose to perform effectively in the slums must work hand-in-glove with the schools, the public housing authority, the police department, the probation department, the courts, the health department, the building inspection department, the human relations department, the employment service, the recreation department, the public assistance agency, and the other private agencies and interest groups operating in the slums. This is a generally accepted principle in social work. It is deficient in practice in very many cities.

A number of the institutions mentioned employ social workers in carrying out their own functions. The public schools, for example, generally have accepted the utility of the school social worker. He used to be called the truant officer and later the visiting teacher. It is the function of the school social worker to follow up on situations outside the school that appear to be impeding a child's progress in school. He sometimes can correct a situation directly, or, if not, marshal the necessary resources to work on the case.

Some public housing authorities employ social workers to handle individual or family problems of tenants or to see that they are referred to the appropriate community agency. Federal housing funds cannot be used for this purpose, as a general rule. Other social workers are sometimes employed for community organization or group work in housing projects.

Many probation officers are trained social workers. Health departments have social service personnel working in tandem with nursing personnel and medical officers, in the recognition that often "health" problems are a mix of "health" and "social," or that a health problem creates accompanying social problems that must be dealt with if any headway is to be made on the health problem.

Probably without exception these services are understaffed in relation to the magnitude and difficulty of the job to be done. Any community serious about tackling its slum problems will add to these staffs and see that social service personnel and agencies work in an integrated fashion in the slums, and do not waste precious energy and resources through competition, cross-purposes, fragmentation, and lack of communication.

Work with families in
deep trouble

The term "multi-problem family" has worked its way into the normal language of people associated with social services. Such a family has so many problems that it seems to be involved with practically all the agencies in town. It is characterized by an apparent almost total incapacity to cope.

Bradley Buell and his associates have analyzed this particular aspect of community life and have found that in cities an overwhelming proportion of the situations, or incidents, or episodes that call for social service originate with a very small number of families.[11]

Often the various agencies that may be dealing with one aspect or another of the multiple problems of these families are unaware of the involvement of the other agencies, or at least do not harmonize their actions with the others. The files on these families grow mountainous and they go on producing more problems.

Buell reasons that these families could be more efficiently

and effectively helped. He suggests essentially two lines of attack. a) *Analysis and classification:* This means surveying caseloads of social agencies (including the public assistance agency, courts, probation, and health services) to find out who these families are and what kinds of problems they present. This is followed by classifying them according to the hierarchy of their problems—which ones are dominant, most pressing, or most powerful in degrading the family. This classification calls for assessment of which families present the greatest potentiality for improvement. b) *Organization and co-ordination.* This entails joint planning and operation by the various agencies involved with the particular family, and assignment of the primary responsibility for the case to one agency (if the dominant problem is one of health, the health agency takes the lead). It also calls for assignment of personnel to the case on the basis of the assessment of probable outcome. If there seem to be possibilities of basic improvement the case will be assigned to the most skilled worker. If all that can be done is a maintenance job, or minimal tasks that must be done to protect the community, even though they may not promise real change in the condition of the family, the case is assigned to a less skilled worker.

This subject is relevant here because it is common knowledge that most multi-problem families live in the slums.

What Buell recommends makes eminent good sense and a number of cities and agencies have organized themselves to function in this way with reference to multi-problem families. It is important to approach these families on a rational and concerted basis because of the intrinsic need of the families themselves, and also because they occasion heavy social and financial costs for the community. They also have the effect of engendering a "problem" atmosphere wherever they are. A teen-age boy in such a family, for example, may be so psychologically disturbed that he becomes the element in a relatively nonviolent street gang that tips it into a source of neighborhood terror. Working to rehabilitate his family thus becomes a measure of prevention.

The criticism that must be made of this approach relates to a sin of omission. The basic analysis that identified the multi-problem family as a social phenomenon and a focus for the organization of social services largely neglected the social context and environmental factors that provide the soil and fertilizer for many of its problems. If the multi-problem families are analyzed in a different way, with attention given to factors outside the intrafamilial ones used almost exclusively in the Buell analysis, some additional perspectives will appear. Such analysis will point to additional strategies of intervention beyond the classification and "family centered case work" that are the central themes of the Buell prescription.

A social, cultural, economic analysis will show that significantly large numbers of multi-problem families are Negro, have very little education, have low skills, live in neighborhoods conducive to deviance from the norms of the larger community, came from poor families originally, and so on. In short, many of these families present characteristics suggesting that attention to a broader arena, beyond the family itself, will be necessary to reduce the number of multi-problem families in the future.

Unfortunately some people have tended to embrace the family centered case work approach as a panacea. This is unfair to the originators of the analysis and detrimental to broader efforts to get at the roots of dependency and disordered behavior. Family centered case work is one important approach to an aspect of the slum problem and should have a place in any comprehensive plan of attack. But it is limited in potential impact and is not the complete solution.

Interpreting the slum to the public and to decision makers

This is an important function that social agencies operating in the slums do not perform well enough now. Too much information material produced by social agencies is limited to interpretation of the services of that particular agency and to making a case for giving it more money. It is a great deal to ask of an agency dependent upon voluntary contributions or legislative appropriations that it present a broad picture and a fundamental analysis in its own propaganda. Yet this is what it is morally obligated to do if it is to continue in good conscience to ask the community for support.

An honest and comprehensive publication about the basic characteristics and situation of its clients may show that that particular agency is not *the* most important agency on the scene, or that it is not the agency with the top priority claim on community resources. It may have a role to play, but this role may be a secondary one. On the day a specialized voluntary agency says: "The first priority is to double the expenditures in the slum schools, then provide resources for our particular function," that agency should get a bonus for statesmanlike behavior.

The need for general knowledge and understanding of conditions in the slums is so great, it is tragic that institutions and agencies with access to this knowledge and competence in interpreting it fail in such large measure to do so. The result is creeping cancer in our cities, the import and extent of which few people are really aware.

Free or low-cost legal services

Poor people are often in trouble with the law because they are poor or because of their ignorance of the law. They lose jobs and income and self-respect and their sense of justice because of the inequities in the operation of laws or the lack of legal counsel.

Poor people are often held in jail for lack of bail when no useful purpose is served by keeping them incarcerated. Not only is no useful purpose served by this, evil purposes are often served because of the frequent loss of employment and the almost inevitable family stress that result. Experiments carried out in New York City by the Vera Foundation have demonstrated that it is not at all necessary to require bail of a great many low income people to insure their appearance in court. Legal counsel or social work personnel are needed to assess each case for recommendation to the judge.

One of the most common difficulties of poor people is that they get in over their heads in installment buying. There are enticing displays of consumer goods and energetic salesmen to encourage this tendency. Often the purchase contracts trouble once they have been caught. This is important in the to fulfill. Legal counsel is needed to advise prospective purchasers in advance of commitment or to help them out of are usurious and almost impossible for the low income person slums because so many people are living at a marginal economic level that excessive charges may sink the ship. This applies to rent as well as to consumer goods.

Many cities have for a long time had well organized legal aid services in operation. These have functioned primarily with reference to marital problems, support payments, custody of children, and indebtedness. A number of states and cities have public defender systems which provide counsel for indigent defendants in criminal cases. Neither of these systems is nearly widespread enough. The late President Kennedy proposed unsuccessfully to Congress in 1963 that the federal government assist in the further development of the public defender system. The need here is evidenced by the fact known to all lawyers that the low income defendant too often has inadequate legal defense.

An important measure in easing one of the troublesome problems of the slum would be to make "preventive" legal counsel available before as well as after the fat is already in the fire on a regular basis in slum neighborhoods. As this is written, New Haven, Connecticut, is experimenting with a system of neighborhood attorneys. Their offices are located in school buildings (which in New Haven are community schools) and they are available for consultation to the people of the neighborhood. They do not handle litigation directly, but refer cases requiring litigation to cooperating attorneys in the city. They do give general and preventive advice, however. Several other cities are planning to install similar systems.

This kind of service would help to avoid legal problems that could be devastating to a poor family, would contribute to the general administration of justice in the area, would inspire a feeling that justice was being protected among the local residents, and would teach the legal profession a great deal about the kinds of problem that beset the low income community.

Health

Much that has been said about social services in the slums can as well be said about health services.

The poor are, more than anyone else, sick and ailing. The infant mortality rates and general morbidity rates in slum areas are a blot on a nation that has advanced in medical science as this one has. For the poor, illness often spells catastrophe, brought on by loss of job and income. To those who live so close to the edge of the cliff, one more step means the end. It is often said that the poor have better medical care available to them than people of middle income because of free clinics. This is not true. In every slum area there is a deficit of preventive and treatment services.

It is obvious that if income and educational levels are raised, health standards will follow. Thus the main thrust along these lines is, in fact, also a public health measure.

Until these better general conditions are approached, there should be no delay in extending more adequate health services in the slums. These will not only save lives, but will also contribute to the greater social and economic health of the area.

One of the basic needs in extending health services in a low income area is for rationalization and coordination with other services, particularly welfare and the schools. This is what happens to a public assistance recipient in New York City:

> If he is ill but able to get about, he goes to an outpatient clinic. If he needs hospitalization he is admitted to a hospital,

but often not at the hospital where he attended the clinic. If he is sick at home or is sent to a nursing home, he is seen by a panel doctor. In each of these instances he will have seen a different physician who usually does not have access to the records of the diagnostic tests and treatments given by the other physicians.

When he is discharged from the hospital he may remain under the supervision of the hospital's home care program, or he may be transferred to the Welfare Department's chronic care programs.

If his illness has resulted in a disability and his prospect of being restored to self-sufficiency are good, he may receive rehabilitation services from the state rehabilitation program, or, if his case is doubtful, he may be sent to a rehabilitation service in a municipal hospital.

If he needs dental care he will be treated in a Welfare Department dental clinic, but if hospitalization is required for a serious dental problem it involves the supervision of a hospital dental service.

Meanwhile his wife may receive her prenatal care in one place and be delivered in another. She may seek attention for her sick children from a clinic and for her well children from a child health station. The younger children in the family will get their dental care from a Health Department clinic, the older ones from a Welfare Department clinic.

With little or no communication between this varied group of services and with a welfare client who may be emotionally upset, with limited education and limited inner resources, the medical care provided will be episodic and uncoordinated, if not chaotic. Welfare clients have been known to develop serious diseases of one part of the body while regularly attending a specialty clinic for the treatment of disease of another part of the body.[12]

This points to the desirability of organizing self-contained comprehensive health units (including mental health) to serve discrete population groupings. This does not mean that all conceivable specialized services and facilities would be available in every unit, since this would be impracticable and prohibitively expensive, not to mention impossible to staff. But each unit would be able to provide comprehensive health care in an integrated fashion, with access to central specialized services when necessary. The services would be organized around the needs of the patients rather than medical specialties and institutional convenience.

It is obvious that our general system of privately financed medical care does not meet the needs of low income groups. To fail to extend adequate health services into the urban areas that need them most is false economy, resulting merely in postponed costs to society and individuals. There is little doubt that most municipalities will be unable to finance adequate health service expansion. In view of this fact of life, state and federal governments should establish systems of financial assistance to local governments for better public health and medical services for people unable to pay the high costs of private medical care. Services could be provided in selected areas low on the socioeconomic scale and high in morbidity and mortality rates, or alternatively, to individuals and families with limited economic resources.

CHAPTER VIII

The Arts

JUST BECAUSE slum residents are all the things the previous pages have said they are does not mean there cannot be a flowering, or at least a budding, of the arts in the slum. This applies both to expression and appreciation. Music, drama, and the plastic arts are unifying forces among men. They help to give a sense of identification with the human race, across national, cultural, ethnic, and other dividing lines. This quality should be recognized and conscious effort made to exploit it in systematic ways to reduce the isolation and alienation of slum people.

Children in slum schools should be exposed to the artistic and cultural resources of the city. This is one of the strong elements of the New York City Higher Horizons Program. This exposure should consist not only of looking and listening, but also of participation (as aides in the museum, backstage workers in the theatre and opera, helpers in the art gallery).

Agencies and institutions should support studios, dramatic

presentations and orchestras in low income areas in which the local residents, young and old alike, can participate.

The idea of coffee shops for teen agers, largely run by them, is a good one. Here they would have not only a place to spend time, but also a back room for music, painting, preparation of shows, and the like. The Mobilization for Youth program in New York provides for an artist-in-residence in one coffee shop and a musician in another.

A museum director in Milwaukee hopes to organize a mobile museum which would move around in the inner city area bringing its treasures right to the people who do not often visit the downtown museum.

The theme here is that the potentialities for artistic creativity are just as great in the slums as anywhere. What is usually lacking is opportunity and stimulus to nurture the potential. Both opportunities for creativity and opportunities to enjoy and benefit from the creative works of others are important in this connection.

EPILOGUE

This is a book without an end.

The day after it is published, someone will develop a new insight or a new perspective on one aspect or another of the slum problem. New ideas for action and policy are being generated constantly. Old forces will be shifting and changing in their influence and unforeseen forces will arise, adding their pressures to the old.

All must be integrated into a mosaic of public and private policy in which the elements are harmonious and in balance. It must be a mosaic without mortar, for the pieces must be changed with changing times. It must be held together by its essential integrity, no one piece or group of pieces dominating the pattern, no one piece achieving its full impress without the others.

Suggestions that have been made in this book may be tried and found wanting, and different ones proposed in their place. The attack on so massive a problem must always provide for this so long as such a developmental process does not divert attention from the major goals or atomize an effort that must be unitary.

Making a difference in slum conditions will require going after the causes of such conditions, not just helping the victims. It will require political support and determination and a high level of professional wisdom.

Most of all it will require the practice of democracy.

NOTES

The author wishes to thank Abingdon Press for permission to reprint from *Songs From the Slums* by Toyohiko Kagawa. Copyright renewal 1963 by Lois J. Erickson.

Notes to Chapter I

1. Eric Partridge, *Origins, A Short Etymological Dictionary of Modern English* (New York: The Macmillan Co., 1958).

2. James B. Conant, *Slums and Suburbs* (New York: McGraw-Hill Book Co., 1961), 7.

3. Reprinted by permission of The World Publishing Company from *The Inhabitants* by Julius Horowitz. Copyright © 1960 by Julius Horowitz.

4. From *How the Other Half Lives* by Jacob Riis. Copyright © 1957 by Hill and Wang, Inc. Riis quotations reprinted by permission of the publisher. (New York: Sagamore Press, 1957), 2.

5. Charles Dickens, *Oliver Twist* (New York: Dodd, Mead & Co., 1941), 74.

6. James Ford, *Slums and Housing: History, Conditions, Policy* (Cambridge: Harvard University Press, 1936), 11.

7. Conference on Home Building and Home Ownership, Washington, D.C., 1931 (quoted in Ford, *ibid.*, 8).

8. *A Primer About Slums* (Albany: New York State Division of Housing, 1958).

9. Herbert Gans, *The Urban Villagers* (New York: The Free Press of Glencoe, 1962).

10. Harry Barnes, *The Slum: Its Story and Solution* (London: P. S. King and Son, 1931), 365.

11. Charles Stokes, "A Theory of Slums," *Land Economics,* Vol. XXXXVIII, No. 3 (August, 1962), pp. 187-97.

12. Michael Harrington, *The Other America* (New York: The Macmillan Co., 1962).

13. John R. Seeley, "The Slum: Its Nature, Use, and Users," *Journal of the American Institute of Planners,* Vol. XXV, No. 1 (February, 1959).

Notes to Chapter II

1. John Kenneth Galbraith, *The Affluent Society* (Boston: Houghton Mifflin Co., 1958), 333.

2. ———— *Wealth and Poverty* (Washington, D.C.: National Policy Committee on Pockets of Poverty, Farmers' Educational Foundation, December, 1963), 3.

3. *Poverty and Deprivation in the United States* (Washington, D.C.: Conference on Economic Progress, 1962).

4. Robert J. Lampman, *The Low Income Population and Economic Growth* (Washington, D.C.: Joint Economic Committee, Congress of the United States, Study Paper No. 12, Dec. 16, 1959).

5. Michael Harrington, *Other America, op. cit.*

6. *The Social Welfare Forum,* Official Proceedings, National Conference on Social Welfare, Minneapolis, May, 1961 (New York: Columbia University Press, 1961), 36-44.

7. International Brotherhood of Teamsters, Joint Council No. 16, news release. (New York: June 11, 1962).

8. *A Social Profile of Detroit* (Ann Arbor: University of Michigan, Department of Sociology and the Survey Research Center of the Institute for Social Research, 1957).

9. Patricia Sexton, *Education and Income* (New York: The Viking Press, 1961).

10. J. N. Morgan, M. H. David, W. S. Cohen, and H. E. Brazer, *Income and Welfare in the United States* (New York: McGraw-Hill Book Co., 1962).

11. Housing and Home Finance Agency, Washington, D.C. A "unit" is a house, apartment, group of rooms, or single room occupied as separate living quarters.

12. *U.S. Census of Housing: 1960* (Washington, D.C.: Department of Commerce, Bureau of the Census), 111.

13. John Robertson, *Housing and Public Health* (New York: Funk & Wagnalls Co., 1920), 181.

14. B. S. Townroe, *The Slum Problem* (New York: Longmans, Green & Co., 1928), 76.

15. Harvey Zorbaugh, *The Gold Coast and The Slums* (Chicago: University of Chicago Press, 1929), 9.

16. Riis, *Other Half, op. cit.,* 13-14.

17. Milovan Djilas, *The New Class, An Analysis of the Communist System* (New York: Frederick A. Praeger, 1957).

18. Walter B. Miller, *Cultural Features of an Urban Lower Class Community* (Washington, D.C.: Community Services Branch, National Institute of Health, 1959).

19. Leonard Reissman, *Class in American Society* (New York: The Free Press of Glencoe, 1959), vii.

20. Frank Riessman, *The Culturally Deprived Child* (New York: Harper & Row, 1962), 26, 27.

21. W. Lloyd Warner, Marcia Meeker, Kenneth Eells, *Social Class in America, the Evaluation of Status* (Chicago: Science Research Associates, 1949).

22. J. A. Kahl, *The American Class Structure* (New York: Holt, Rinehart & Winston, 1957).

23. Oscar Lewis, *The Children of Sanchez* (New York: Random House, 1963), XXV.

24. Richard Cloward, "Private Social Welfare and The Poor" (unpublished ms.).

25. Charles V. Willie and Morton O. Wagenfeld, *Socio-Economic and Ethnic Areas of Syracuse and Onondaga County, 1960* (Syracuse: Youth Development Center, Syracuse University, 1962).

26. *Indices of Social Problems* (New York: New York City Youth Board, 1962).

27. Alvin L. Schorr, *Slums and Social Insecurity* (Washington: Department of Health, Education, and Welfare, 1963), 31.

28. Ralph Ellison, *The Invisible Man* (New York: Signet Books, 1947), 7.

29. Daniel Katz and Kenneth Braly, "Verbal Stereotypes and Racial Prejudice," in Guy Swanson, *et al.,* eds., *Readings in Social Psychology* (New York: Holt, Rinehart & Winston, 1952), 44.

30. Harry Sharp and Leo Schnore, "The Changing Color Composition of Metropolitan Areas," *Journal of Land Economics,* Vol. XXXVIII, No. 2 (May, 1962).

31. Charles Silberman, "The City and the Negro," *Fortune* (March, 1962).

32. Morton Grodzins, *The Metropolitan Area as a Racial Problem* (Pittsburgh: University of Pittsburgh Press, 1958).

33. *Ibid.* These four general rules were formulated by Grodzins.

34. *Where Shall We Live?* Report of the Commission on Race and Housing (Berkeley: University of California Press, 1958), 4.

35. Robert C. Weaver, *The Negro Ghetto* (New York: Harcourt, Brace and World, 1948), viii.

36. St.Clair Drake and Horace R. Cayton, *Black Metropolis: A Study of Negro Life in a Northern City* (New York: Harcourt, Brace & World, 1945), 9.

37. Irving Shulman, *West Side Story* (New York: Pocket Books, Inc., 1961), 6.

38. Patricia Sexton, *Education, op. cit.*

39. *Ibid.*

40. *Ibid.*, p. 26.

41. Margaret Greenfield, *Social Dependency* (Berkeley: University of California Press, 1963).

42. *A Proposal for the Prevention and Control of Delinquency by Expanding Opportunities* (New York: Mobilization For Youth, Inc., December 9, 1961), 25.

43. *Income, Education, and Employment in Neighborhoods* (Washington, D.C.: Dept. of Labor, Bureau of Labor Statistics, January, 1963).

44. Manhattanville Community Centers, Inc. memorandum (New York: April, 1963).

45. *A Community Action Program for Youth* (Cleveland: Greater Cleveland Youth Service Planning Commission, December, 1962).

46. Charles Willie and Morton Wagenfeld, *Syracuse, op. cit.*

47. *Atlanta's People* (Atlanta: Community Council of the Atlanta Area, January, 1963).

48. Irving A. Spergel and Richard E. Mundy, *A Community Study —East Woodlawn: Problems, Programs, Proposals* (Chicago: School of Social Service Administration, University of Chicago, March, 1963).

49. Tabulation of Action for Boston Community Development (April, 1963).

50. City of New York, Department of Welfare, September, 1962.

51. Charles H. Tenney, testimony before sub-committee on Em-

ployment and Manpower, U.S. Senate Committee on Labor and Public Welfare (August, 15, 1963).

52. *Community Action Program for Youth* (Greater Cleveland Youth Service Planning Commission, 1962).

53. Cleveland Board of Education, Bureau of Educational Research, memorandum (1962).

54. Sophonisba P. Breckenridge and Edith Abbott, *The Delinquent Child and the Home* (New York: Russell Sage Foundation, 1912.

55. Clifford Shaw and Henry D. McKay, *Delinquency Areas* (Chicago: University of Chicago Press, 1929).

56. Edwin H. Sutherland, *Principles of Criminology* (Chicago: J. B. Lippincott Co., 1924).

57. Gus Tyler, *Organized Crime in America* (Ann Arbor: University of Michigan Press, 1962), 83.

58. See Richard O. Cloward and Lloyd Ohlin, *Delinquency and Opportunity* (New York: The Free Press of Glencoe, 1960) for an explanation of differential access to "legitimate" and "illegitimate" opportunities.

59. R. B. Navin, *Analysis of a Slum Area in Cleveland* (Cleveland Metropolitan Housing Authority, 1934).

60. "Final Report to Honorable Frank P. Zeidler, Mayor, City of Milwaukee" (Milwaukee: Study Committee on Social Problems in the Inner Core of the City, 1960).

61. Albert J. Reiss, Jr., and Albert Lewis Rhodes, *A Sociopsychological Study of Conforming and Deviating Behavior Among Adolescents* (Washington, D.C.: U.S. Office of Education, Cooperative Research Project 507, 1959).

62. *Indices of Social Problems* (New York: New York City Youth Board, 1960).

63. Thomas S. Langner and Stanley T. Michael, *Life Stress and Mental Health* (New York: The Free Press of Glencoe, 1963).

64. Allison Davis and John Dollard, *Children of Bondage* (Washington, D.C.: American Council on Education, 1940), 266.

65. Martin Deutsch and Bert Brown, *Some Data on Social Influences in Negro-White Intelligence Differences* (New York: Institute for Developmental Studies, Department of Psychiatry, New York Medical College, 1963), 8.

66. *Selected Population Characteristics of West Side Urban Renewal Area, Manhattan: Census of 1960* (New York: Bureau of Com-

munity Statistical Services, Community Council of Greater New York, January, 1963).

67. *A Primer About Slums and Urban Renewal, op. cit.*

68. Patricia Sexton, *Education, op. cit.,* 253, 254.

69. Alfred J. Kahn, *Planning Community Services for Children in Trouble* (New York: Columbia University Press, 1963), 12.

70. Reviewed in Ruth L. Mace, *Municipal Cost-Revenue Research in the United States* (Chapel Hill: University of North Carolina, Institute of Government, 1961).

71. Robert B. Navin, *Analysis of a Slum Area* (Washington, D.C.: Catholic University of America, 1934).

72. *Urban Land Policy* (St. Louis City Plan Commission, 1936).

73. Jay Rumney and Sara Shuman, *The Cost of Slums in Newark* (Newark: Housing Authority of the City of Newark, 1946).

74. John C. Alston, *Cost of a Slum Area* (Wilberforce, Ohio: Wilberforce State College, 1948).

75. Donald J. Bogue, *Skid Row in American Cities* (Chicago: Community and Family Study Center, University of Chicago, 1963).

76. *The Homeless Men on Skid Row* (Chicago: Tenants Relocation Bureau, City of Chicago, 1961).

77. Robert M. MacIver, *The Ramparts We Guard* (New York: The Macmillan Co., 1950), 18.

78. Harold Lasswell, "The Threat to Privacy" in Robert MacIver, ed., *Conflict of Loyalties* (New York: Harper & Row, 1952), 132.

79. Leo Srole, "Social Integration and Certain Corollaries," *American Sociological Review,* Vol. 21, No. 6 (December, 1956), 712-13.

80. Harvey W. Zorbaugh, *The Gold Coast and the Slums* (Chicago: University of Chicago Press, 1929), 9.

81. See *A Proposal for the Prevention and Control of Delinquency by Expanding Opportunities, op. cit.,* for a good summary discussion of this subject.

Notes to Chapter III

1. James B. Conant, *Slums and Suburbs* (New York: McGraw-Hill Book Co., 1961), 2.

2. Robert J. Havighurst, "Educating the Children of Our Slums," *New City,* Vol. I, No. 17 (February 1, 1963), 9-12.

3. A. Harry Passow, ed., *Education in Depressed Areas* (New York: Columbia University Press, 1963).

4. Robert C. Weaver, *Urban Planning Problems*. Los Angeles, address to American Orthopsychiatric Association, March 22, 1962.

5. George W. Burchill, *Work Study Programs for Alienated Youth: A Casebook* (Chicago: Science Research Associates, 1962).

6. Dewitt Hunt, *Work Experience Education Programs in American Schools* (Washington, D.C.: Department of Health, Education, and Welfare, Bulletin No. 5, 1957).

7. Robert J. Havighurst and Lindley J. Stiles, "A Statement of National Policy for Alienated Youth," *Phi Delta Kappan* (April, 1961).

8. Robert J. Havighurst, "The Urban Lower Class School," *Human Development Symposium* (University of Chicago, April, 1962).

9. Robert J. Havighurst, "Educating the Children of Our Slums," *New City*, Vol. 1, No. 17 (February, 1963), 9-12.

10. *Ibid.*

11. Henry Saltzman, *Racial Imbalances in Big City School Systems*. Denver, address to National School Boards Association, April 28, 1963.

12. *Ibid.*

13. James B. Conant, *Slums and Suburbs, op. cit.*, 147.

14. S. M. Miller, *Dropouts—A Political Problem*. Washington, D.C., working paper presnted at Symposium on School Dropouts, National Education Association, December 2-4, 1962.

15. *Ibid.*

Notes to Chapter V

1. Robert Dahl, *Who Governs?* (New Haven: Yale University Press, 1961).

2. Warren E. Miller, *Participation in Elections: The Problem* (Ann Arbor: University of Michigan, Industrial Relations Research Association, Survey Research Center, 1960).

3. Donald E. Stokes, *Voting Research and the Business Man in Politics* (Ann Arbor: The Foundation for Research on Human Behavior, 1960).

4. William G. Mather, "Income and Social Participation," *American Sociological Review*, Vol. 6, No. 3 (June, 1941), pp. 380-81.

5. These four reasons for nonparticipation are presented in "A Proposal for the Prevention and Control of Delinquency by Expanding Opportunities" (New York: Mobilization for Youth, Inc., 1961), 126-31.

6. Warren Haggstrom, informal memo to "Anyone Interested," Youth Development Center, Syracuse University, (April 28, 1963).

7. Lloyd Ohlin, "Issues in the Development of Indigenous Social Movements Among Residents of Deprived Urban Areas." Unpublished memo prepared for the Ford Foundation (October, 1960).

8. Saul Alinsky, quoted in "Plan of Operations, Neighborhood Urban Extension" (Pittsburgh: ACTION Housing, Inc., 1963). See also Saul Alinsky, *Reveille for Radicals* (Chicago: University of Chicago Press, 1946).

9. Warren G. Haggstrom, memo. Youth Development Center, Syracuse University (October 16, 1962).

10. Lloyd Ohlin, *Issues in the Development, op. cit.*

11. Saul Alinsky, *Reveille for Radicals, op. cit.*, 204.

12. Richard and Hephzibah Hauser, *The Fraternal Society* (New York: Random House, 1962), 90.

13. Nicholas von Hoffman, "Reorganization of the Casbah," *Social Progress*, Vol. 3, No. 6 (April, 1962), p. 33.

14. Carl Feiss, "Urban Renewal: Running Hard and Sitting Still" *Architectural Forum*, Vol. 116 No. 4 (April, 1962), p. 183.

15. S. M. Miller, "Social Action Programs: Some Questions." Unpublished memo, Youth Development Center, Syracuse University (April, 1963).

16. Nicholas von Hoffman, "Reorganization of the Casbah," *op. cit.*

17. Herbert Gans, review of Peter H. Rossi and Robert A. Dentler, *The Politics of Urban Renewal: The Chicago Findings*, in *Commentary* (February, 1963).

18. W. Lloyd Warner, *Social Class in America* (New York: Harper & Row, 1949), 24.

19. Mobilization for Youth, *A Proposal, op. cit.*, 322.

Notes to Chapter VI

1. Harry Barnes, *The Slum: Its Story and Solution* (London: P. S. King and Son, Ltd., 1931).

2. Robert C. Weaver, personal communication. Housing and Home Finance Agency, Washington, D.C. (December, 1962).

3. Martin Meyerson, Barbara Terrett, and William L. C. Wheaton, *Housing, People, and Cities* (New York: McGraw-Hill Book Co., 1962), 16.

4. For a good summary of the directions in which state governments might move, see Edward C. Banfield and Morton Grodzins, *Government and Housing in Metropolitan Areas* (New York: McGraw-Hill Book Co., 1958).

5. Raymond Vernon, *Anatomy of a Metropolis* (Cambridge: Harvard University Press, 1959).

6. Thomas F. Johnson, James R. Morris, and Joseph G. Butts, *Renewing America's Cities* (Washington, D.C.: The Institute for Social Science Research, 1962).

7. *Ibid.*, p. 116.

8. Martin Meyerson *et al.*, *Housing, People, and Cities, op. cit.*, 32.

9. E. A. Gutkind, *The Twilight of Cities* (New York: The Free Press of Glencoe, 1962) 173.

10. "Today's Decisions, Tomorrow's Problems" (New York: Regional Plan Association, April, 1963).

11. Survey by The Western Real Estate Research Corporation.

12. James Baldwin, *Nobody Knows My Name* (New York: Dell Books, 1961), 60.

13. "A Clearer Focus," Annual Report of the New York City Housing Authority (1962).

14. New York Regional Office, Public Housing Administration, press release (July 22, 1963), 2.

15. "The New Look in Public Housing—Too Little and Too Late?" *Architectural Forum* (July, 1963), 116.

16. "Successful Experiment—The Used House Program," *Issues* (Philadelphia Housing Association, April, 1963), 1.

17. Robert C. Weaver, address to American Orthopsychiatric Association, Los Angeles (March 22, 1962).

18. "The Community Renewal Program: The First Years" (Chicago: American Society of Planning Officials, 1963).

19. Jane Jacobs, *The Death and Life of Great American Cities* (New York: Random House, 1961).

20. Paul Ylvisaker, *Community Action: A Response to Some Unfinished Business* (New York: The Ford Foundation, 1963).

Notes to Chapter VII

1. Bertram Beck, personal communication. National Association of Social Workers, 1963.

2. *Ibid.*

3. Nathan Cohen, personal communication. 1964 National Conference on Social Welfare, 1963.

4. Roy Sorenson, personal communication. Metropolitan San Francisco YMCA, 1962.

5. Richard Cloward, personal communication. Columbia School of Social Work, 1963.

6. "Recommendations for New Eastern High School and Family Center" (Detroit Public Schools, mimeographed, January, 1963).

7. "A Social Plan for Homewood Brushton" (Pittsburgh: Health and Welfare Association of Allegheny County (March, 1963), 23.

8. Irving A. Spergel and Richard E. Mundy, "A Community Study, East Woodlawn: Problems, Programs, Proposals" (Chicago: School of Social Service Administration, University of Chicago, dittoed, March, 1963), 93.

9. Frank Riessman, "New Models for a Treatment Approach to Low Income Clients," paper presented at American Orthopsychiatric Association, Washington, D.C. (March 8, 1963).

10. Herbert Gans, *The Urban Villagers* (New York: The Free Press of Glencoe, 1962) 98.

11. Bradley Buell *et al., Community Planning for Human Services* (New York: Columbia University Press, 1952).

12. Leona Baumgartner and James R. Dumpson, "Health in Welfare: A Joint or a Divided Responsibility?" *American Journal of Public Health,* Vol. 52, No. 7, pp. 1067-76 (July, 1962). Dr. Baumgartner at the time was Commissioner of Health of New York City and Mr. Dumpson, Commissioner of Welfare.